HOW TO PASS YOUR MOTORCYCLE TEST FIRST TIME

by Stuart Miller

foulsham

LONDON • NEW YORK • TORONTO • SYDNEY

foulsham

The Publishing House, Bennetts Close, Cippenham, Berkshire, SL1 5AP, England

ISBN 0-572-02225-5

This book is dedicated to Martin, who left too early and should still be here, and Andy whose assistance and companionship I have come to value over the recent year.

Typeset by Poole Typesetting (Wessex) Ltd, Bournemouth.
Printed in Great Britain by Cox & Wyman Ltd, Reading, Berkshire.

CONTENTS

PREFACE

I have written this book because none of the inordinate number of other motorcycle instruction manuals around with titles like 'How to pass your bike test' seemed to fulfilled that promise. They told you how to ride and explained all about the mechanics of a machine, but none ever got remotely near telling you how to pass the bike test, or gave any serious detail about what to expect on it. To say also that many of these books appear to be written in a somewhat 'dry' style would be a bit of an understatement. They'd convince me, if I was new to motorcycling, that bikers are devoid of any sense of humour – and learning to ride a bike can be a very amusing experience, not least for your instructor.

I know what you want. It was not so long ago that I learnt to ride myself, so I can remember the nerves and the desire to know more about what happened during the test before I actually took it - information I was unable to get either from the school where I learnt to ride or from books.

This book should be read in conjunction with the training that you receive at an approved training school. You cannot learn to ride a motorbike from a book. What I hope I can do is to prepare you in advance of taking a training course, so that you have an idea of what to expect.

To set the general tone of this book, may I suggest you equate learning to ride a bike with sex. Always be aware of what's going on behind you, take plenty of precautions, by all means dress up in leather if that's your wont, grip tightly with your thighs and keep mentally alert but relaxed – the more you do, the more you'll enjoy it.

Motorcycling is dangerous. Actually, I don't believe it is but I just thought I'd say that to get you all wound up. However, it has to be said that a great many people do believe this to be the case. If a car driver jumps a red light and smacks into a motorcyclist passing through a junction, then there can be no argument that the chances of survival on a bike are considerably less than they might be in a car. Motorcycling isn't dangerous, motorcyclists are simply more vulnerable. If you are taught well, then you will be taught to ride defensively and to take nothing for granted. So when your traffic light turns to green and you set off, you will still have a quick glance to your left and right as you pass through the junction, just to be absolutely sure there's nothing there.

It would be wrong of me to deny that riders get hurt. It's not just a question of getting hit by a car – you can fall off for reasons that are often beyond your control – running into a patch of diesel for example. You can stack the odds in your favour by taking the correct initial training. If you mix with bikers, you will, sooner or later, hear of someone who's been injured or even killed riding a motorbike. You will certainly read about it from time to time. But that honestly doesn't mean it will necessarily happen to you or that it is inevitable that you will fall off. What it does mean is that you must always concentrate and constantly apply the techniques you have been taught in training.

Motorcycling comes as a shock to most people, particularly car drivers who decide to give it a go. Suddenly, they realise they have to wake up, think about their riding and be conscious of what they're doing all the time.

I reckon motorcyclists are touched with a brush of eccentricity – others might even say we are a bit odd. It has to be admitted that it is a bit of a selfish pursuit. While most bikes can carry a passenger, riding a bike is generally a solo activity. One doesn't necessarily have to equate selfishness with eccentricity, but if you stare at your riding colleagues you will notice that while many are dull and boring, many also are different – extraordinary in its truest sense.

Why do it? Because it's fun, because you need to do it to get to work, because it's a challenge, because you're sick of traffic jams and train strikes, because you're a criminal and need a quick means of escape. You don't need an excuse. I have my own reasons. I've used my motorcycle to get to work and to go on business trips, I've gone on holiday on it and I regularly use it to get to football matches. It's used to teach others to ride and for simple enjoyment. It is often a real thrill.

One of the biggest pluses is the ability of a bike to get me to my destination as quickly as I choose without having to worry about traffic jams. Driving on Britain's roads in the 90s is something that depresses me deeply. Public highways are now dreadfully overcrowded and travellers subjected to frequent and sudden delays. But it really is better by bike. With proper care and skill, you are able to scythe through queues of traffic. The biggest danger is getting smug.

An interesting subject. Undoubtedly, most people either go to one they've picked out of Yellow Pages or to one a mate has recommended. Is there anything wrong with that? Not necessarily, if it all works out fine for you in the end. If most potential trainees are honest, when they've decided that they want to learn to ride a bike, all they're really interested in is getting that pass ticket off the examiner and they're not too bothered how they get there. If there are shortcomings in their training, people tend to believe they're bright enough to sort them out for themselves when they're on the road for real.

Some of you reading the above paragraph will have bristled at what I've written and insist that while certainly you want to pass your test, you also want to be taught to ride a motorcycle properly. This section of the book is for you.

There are those who question whether they need to take full training at all. Compulsory Basic Training (CBT) is mandatory and without the DL 196 certificate you can not take your test. Training after CBT is optional. As someone who owns a training school I have a vested interest in persuading people to take further training but I would put it to you that your chances of passing are severely reduced without it. Bear in mind that the examiner doesn't just expect to see you ride, he also expects to see you ride to the prescribed system. You could get a mate who's done it to explain it to you and you might get away with it if you're fairly bright and lucky too. But you might not.

It's all very well me listing the criteria which will help you select your training school, but if you live in an area where there is little choice then it's a fait accompli. If you are in this situation where for geographical reasons there is only one logical choice, then so be it. It could be a good place to learn to ride a bike. It probably will be. Go there with a positive attitude and if you do find shortcomings, then I hope that this book will plug the gaps. I should also be honest enough to say that what you are about to read are my opinions, as indeed is the whole philosophy of this book. Show this marvellous example of literary genius to another expert and he may disagree quite vehemently with much of what I say. Of course he'd be wrong, but the point I'm making is that this other expert may give you equally sound reasons as to why a particular training school is good when I might suggest it isn't. In any specialist subject, so-called experts often disagree. Ego might have something to do with it. But in the end of course, it's your choice.

I would describe motorcycle training schools (ATBs as I will now refer to them – Approved Training Bodies) as falling into two camps: full-time and part-time. The essential difference is that full-time ATBs will usually offer CBT seven days a week while part-timers will only offer it perhaps on weekends. The road training that follows on after CBT may also be more restricted at a part-time school. You may well have gathered by now that I have my own training school and I would classify it as a part-time operation. I do Compulsory Basic Training (CBT) on weekends only, but offer road training six days a week.

I am speaking very generally now, but part-timers are usually people who have another job and give their spare time to

training. While the vast majority of all instructors are dedicated to the job and do it because they love it, part-timers tend to be more dedicated and committed. They can also often be dull boring people without any sparkle or imagination or sense of humour when it comes to teaching. Not all, I must stress, but definitely some. They will certainly tend to be very thorough.

Full-timers tend to be driven by factors other than just a desire to turn out a constant succession of competent riders. The principal factor is, er …, money. They're running a business with the profit motive being the bottom line. However, they will be spending more time actually teaching.

I should point out to you that ATBs are subject to checks by the Driving Standards Agency. I would like to have said that they're subject to frequent checks. The DSA is also a victim of the realities of economics and when they send someone along to inspect an ATB, particularly on a weekend, they're paying heavy money out in overtime. In July 1996, in my area, they are restricting visits to three hours, and we get a visit about once every three to four months. Nevertheless, rest assured that there are quality control checks done on ATBs on a regular basis, to make sure that they're doing what they should be doing, and that their standards are high and consistent. Make no mistake, if an inspector (who is usually an examiner) sees something that he doesn't like, he will take steps to get it changed, and the DSA have the ultimate sanction of being able to shut a place down. Anyone with a full bike licence can become an instructor. If an individual has held a licence for under two years, he is restricted to the off-road element of CBT. In other words, he cannot accompany someone for the road ride part of the CBT course. There is a loophole however which I will cover shortly. Somebody in this position is called an Assistant Instructor. Anyone with a licence held in excess of two years can do the lot and they are simply known as Instructors. However, all these instructors, no matter what their title or status, have to be trained to teach. The responsibility for training all the instructors is down to the big boss man, the Chief Instructor. Each ATB will have at least one and he will have been away on a brief residential course at the DSA's training headquarters. The buck stops with him or her.

So, back to the point at hand. You want to learn to ride a bike and you haven't got a clue which training school is best. To start with, where do you look? The most obvious place is the Yellow Pages or with your local version of the Thompson Directory. You can also try the classified ads in Motor Cycle News or the display ads in many of the glossy bike magazines.

Drawn a blank? Then try the Road Safety Officer at the town hall, your local bike dealer, or the British Motorcyclists Federation (01825 712896), use your own initiative!

So, you've come up with one, maybe two or three names. Which one? Well, if a friend pushes you in the direction of a particular one because they went there and were happy, why shouldn't you go there too? Is your friend sane? Do you trust their judgement? Likewise, if they're saying, 'Don't go to that one, I went there and they were rubbish', get specific reasons as to why that was the case. Ring them all anyway, and ask the following appropriate questions:

'I HAVE NEVER RIDDEN A BIKE BEFORE AND I WANT TO BE TRAINED UP TO TAKE AND PASS MY BIKE TEST. HOW MUCH!?'

The reply will depend on how quickly you want to do it. Large training schools offer intensive or, as I prefer to call them, crash courses, where, depending on your previous experience, you can start on a Monday and take your test on Friday. In July 1996, prices for a five day course will range from £300 to £400. These five day courses are for complete novices but these schools will also offer two or three day courses for people who have some previous experience, and the prices will drop accordingly.

My main reservation about these courses is that I believe it is too short a period in which to learn to ride a bike properly. Lots of people have gone on them and passed their tests and I think most of them are still riding around. But I believe that people need time to absorb what they've learnt between lessons on perhaps a weekly basis, and a few hours between rides is not long enough.

The alternative to an intensive course is one where you're brought back on a weekly basis. These schemes are probably the most popular of all and are highly effective, successful, and also considerably cheaper. For this type of course you should be looking to pay approximately £200. Training will be more relaxed and spread out over a few weeks but if you happen to be in a hurry, these too can be speeded up with the co-operation of your ATB.

'HOW LONG DOES TRAINING TAKE?'

If you can, avoid ATBs which quote you a price for a fixed period of training. They might say it's so much for CBT and three on-the-road training sessions for example. Fine, but what happens after those three on-the-road sessions if you're not up to the test standard? 'Oh, well, we charge you £15 per hour for further training.' On that basis, you might as well give them a blank cheque.

The same applies to intensive courses. What happens if after five days you're not up to it? Ask and find out how much extra, if anything, it will cost. Ideally, you want a fixed price for as much training as you'll need to get you through the test.

If you're an average novice, you'll be looking at approximately four to seven road sessions before you'll be approaching test standard. But don't be too disheartened if you take a lot longer. There are tremendous variations. You'll begin to realise yourself as your training progresses, how good you are and how much more work you need to do.

'IS BIKE HIRE INCLUDED IN THE PRICE?'

This is a very important point and is a factor that many do not consider properly. These days, you do not need to have your own machine for training purposes and the first motorbike you buy should be the one you get after you've passed your test. Any reputable training school will have bikes to hire out. However, some people still think that they would be better off with their own machine as it means that they can practise in between lessons. By all means get your own bike if you can afford it, and with the scarcity of good second-hand 125 cc bikes around these days, you're quite likely to get your money back when you come to sell it later. However, I do not believe it is necessary to have your own machine to practise on. It doesn't seem to make any difference to the majority of my trainees.

Bike hire though can be a major source of income to ATBs and can make the final costs of what looks like a very reasonably priced training course very expensive. You should be able to get a training course which includes as much training as you'll need, with bike hire thrown in, for a fixed one-off price. Otherwise, you'll be charged anything from £10 to £20 each time you ride the blessed thing, and then you might also get stung with an additional charge for insurance. Sort out the details first and you are less likely to get a nasty surprise later.

'IS THE TEST FEE INCLUDED IN THE PRICE?'

With some it is, with some it isn't. Again you need to establish this fact if finance is important to you. As previously mentioned, at the time of writing (July 1996) the fee is £36.

'WHEN DO YOU DO CBT AND HOW LONG DOES IT TAKE?'

CBT is the first thing you'll do when you commence your training, no matter what your licence status. Most training schools try and get through it in a day. Have you got a day in your schedule to give up? If so, does the ATB do it on a day that is convenient for you?

Some part-time training schools spread it out over perhaps two or three weekends, maybe doing two hours at a time. Their prices may be cheaper, but is that too slow and drawn out for you?

I believe it is perfectly reasonable for most people to get through CBT in one day, although as mentioned before, not everyone manages it and it can be very exhausting. The next day you should expect the odd muscle twinge or ache.

There are some people who only want to do CBT and not take further training for the time being, either because they can't afford it, or in the case of 16 year olds, because they want to wait till they're 17 and can proceed from a moped on to a motorbike.

If CBT is all you want, again make sure that the price you pay is as inclusive as possible. Some places offer two prices – a higher one for a guaranteed pass and a lower one that does not guarantee a pass. On the latter there is potential for ripping you off on the excuse that you are not up to the required standard on a particular exercise and need to come back for further training at so much an hour. Beware!

One last point on this particular subject. An instructor is allowed to oversee four pupils when conducting the off-road element of CBT but only two when taking them out on the road ride part of the course Make sure that the ATB sticks to this and you don't find for example that you've got one instructor with more than four trainees. There is one exception to this rule. Holders of a full car licence issued before December 1990 need not be counted for the purpose of

student/instructor ratios. This will change, however, from July 1 1996.

'AFTER CBT, HOW MANY OTHER TRAINEES WILL THERE BE WITH ME ON ROAD RIDE TRAINING?'

There is a fair amount of controversy about this point at the moment because in July 1994, a trainee was killed while on the road with a training school. This prompted a national debate on this subject. And it is frequently in this area where the differences between a full-time commercial organisation and a less profit-motivated part-time one surface.

Road ride training is where you go out on the road with an instructor, put into practice what you've learnt on your CBT and develop your riding skills further until you're accomplished enough to take your test. You will probably have seen the little gaggles of learners about often referred to as ducklings on account of the fact that they're frequently in a meticulous line, all following one another.

Unlike the CBT course, there are no restrictions as to how many pupils an instructor is permitted to supervise when out on the road except on Direct Access where the ratio is 2:1. Clearly it is more economically efficient to have one instructor controlling as many learners as he can. On this matter you are in the hands of the ATB and are dependent upon them being responsible.

The largest commercial training body in the UK has a policy of taking out five trainees per instructor. I have heard stories of other training schools with considerably more pupils than that to one instructor. Obviously, there could be serious

safety implications involved. There can be no question that an ATB has a clear duty of responsibility to its customers to do its best to ensure their safety. Speaking for myself, I am just about happy enough supervising three. With that number and with me doing my job as I should, I feel I can safely watch everyone at the same time and have proper control and discipline over the ride. Some people feel that the maximum should be two or even one pupil to an instructor. There is some merit in these arguments.

So ask this question of your potential ATB and await the response. If it's fudged or if the number appears high, then no matter how attractive a financial proposition they may appear to be, think again.

'DO YOU USE RADIOS ON ROAD TRAINING?'

Quite frankly, I just wouldn't consider a school that doesn't use them. It is a basic piece of equipment for an ATB that does much to enhance safety. If they can't stump up the cash to buy a few sets I feel they can't be serious about what they're doing.

'WHAT HAPPENS IF I FAIL MY TEST?'

You should be told that all further training will be free. You should also be told in fact that there are no further charges, period. No bike hire charges, nothing except the test fee itself.

'DO I GET A LESSON IMMEDIATELY BEFORE MY TEST?'

You should certainly expect one, ideally immediately before your test for perhaps an hour or so. Not too much longer as you don't want to be tired when going into the test. Just nicely warmed up.

'WILL MY INSTRUCTOR ACCOMPANY ME TO THE TEST CENTRE AND WAIT?'

He might well accompany you but he probably won't wait. Do you mind? Would you rather be on your own? It's an indication of the school's commitment to you if the instructor will wait and debrief you afterwards but don't be too surprised if the answer to this question is 'no'.

'I'M VERTICALLY CHALLENGED. WILL YOU HAVE A BIKE I CAN CLIMB ON?'

If you are very short then you may never be truly comfortable, no matter what bike they give you. But it is worth asking. 125 cc machines can vary tremendously in size and and a seat a few inches lower can make all the difference to your comfort – and safety.

'I'M A WOMAN AND I WANT TO BE TAUGHT BY A WOMAN. DO YOU HAVE FEMALE INSTRUCTORS?'

I've never been asked about this but I'm aware that one or two ATBs do make an issue of it and advertise the fact that they employ female instructors. If this is an issue that does

concern you then of course ask but be prepared for a negative answer. Female motorcycle instructors are not thick on the ground, although they certainly exist, and one or two ATBs have started running women-only courses.

You will notice that throughout this book I refer to instuctors, examiners and riders as 'he'. This should of course be taken to mean 'he' or 'she'.

'I HAVEN'T GOT A HELMET OR OTHER EQUIPMENT. CAN YOU LEND ME SOME?'

The answer should be 'yes' and there should be no charge. Virtually every school lends out helmets and many offer other items too, like gloves and waterproofs. However, you don't know how that helmet may have been treated or looked after and it's always possible it's not worth the polycarbonate it's made out of. If you can afford it, on top of the cost of the training etc., then do buy your own.

Even after you have asked all of that lot, you may still have some unanswered questions, such as:

'SHOULD I CHOOSE AN INSTRUCTOR WHO SOUNDED DISINTERESTED?'

In this day and age, it is reasonable for you to assume that if any business wishes to give the impression of being professional in its approach, then they will ensure that their first point of contact with their potential customers is handled by someone who is polite, friendly, helpful and sounds as if he is interested in you and keen for your custom. If that is not the case then you may well come to the conclusion that the business is either owned or run by cretins, or that it is so successful that they couldn't care less if they miss one or two punters through incompetence. Either way, is it the right place for you and your hard-earned cash?

On the other hand, there are some who might well be brilliant instructors but who might not be able to even remember their own name let alone be a fit and proper person to be in charge of a commercial concern. It can be a hard decision, particularly if the company you happen to be speaking to and asking questions of is the only choice you've got for near-on 50 miles.

And finally

'I'VE ASKED ALL THE QUESTIONS AND THE ANSWERS ARE MIXED. WHAT DO I DO?'

It depends how far you're prepared to compromise. If the person you're asking all these questions of is giving you honest replies, then at least that's something, even if they're not the answers you wanted. To be frank, I'd be surprised if you got the hoped-for response to every question. What I've listed would be the ideal but none of us is perfect and although most try hard to give the type of service they in turn would like to receive, there will inevitably be shortcomings in every set up. The important thing is that you are taught well, taught safely, and that you enjoy it.

In closing this chapter, I would like to apologise to you for turning what might at first have seemed an uncomplicated and joyous prospect into a version of the Krypton Factor. But it's a hard and nasty world where there are sharks aplenty just waiting to remove wads of cash from your wallet.

There are two stages in the process of becoming a full motorcycle licence holder. First is Compulsory Basic Training or CBT. This must be conducted by a recognised and approved training body (ATB). It includes lessons on theory, basic machine control and manoeuvres carried out on private land away from traffic, and finally a ride on public roads. CBT was introduced in December 1990.

From January 1997, you must take CBT before you ride on the road. You cannot even ride your bike to the training centre, if you happen to have your own machine, to attend the course. You have to get it there by other means.

I need to stress one thing about the CBT course itself. There is a prescribed syllabus which each training school must follow, but as long as the points are covered, then each school has a certain limited amount of latitude as to how it approaches teaching. All I can do here is relate to you how I teach it. When you go for training, it may seem quite different. There is a tendency to believe that because something is in a book, then anything that book says on a particular point is always right and anybody else's opinions or ideas are wrong. This is not so. If there appears at any time to be a serious conflict between the way I describe something and the way your instructor does, then by all means question your instructor but if he gives you what sounds like a plausible response, then follow his methods.

A note of clarification at this point. I have referred often during the course of this book to CBT being done 'off-road'. This does not mean that you traipse off into a field and ride trail bikes. All it means is that you are on a properly surfaced area, like a car park, which is not part of the public road system, so that you can train in obvious safety.

On the day of your CBT course, be alert and ready. Wake up properly, open the curtains, and look outside. Is it raining? Is it cold? Then dress accordingly.

You can't afford proper motorcycling clothing? No problem. If it's winter then put on more layers of underclothing than you would in summer. Starting at the bottom, don't wear trainers, no matter what season. Put on a tough pair of boots or if you haven't got any, as strong a pair of shoes as you can manage. Wear thick socks, particularly in winter. If you've got long johns or wear ladies' tights, then put 'em on over which should go as durable a pair of trousers as you can manage. In nine cases out of ten, that means denim jeans but they're not very good on their own. The thing is, I'm not just dressing you to keep you warm and dry. You should always assume when you climb on a bike, that halfway into your journey you're going to fall off. That's a cheery note to start your course on, isn't it? So what can you put on to protect yourself? Jeans will suffice if you can wear something else over them. Finish it off with a strong jacket which ideally should be waterproof. If it's not, bring waterproof clothing. And don't forget gloves – any type will be better than nothing.

You may find this hard to imagine, but even on a warm summer's day there will still be a 'chill' factor when you're riding along. It won't necessarily be unpleasant but just

recognise the fact that it will be cooler when you're moving. Remember this: if you put on too much clothing and find you're uncomfortably warm, then you can take it off, can't you? But if you're too cold ...

If you've booked with a nice friendly place, the first thing they should do besides taking your money is to sit you down and ply you with coffee or tea. That is, if there is somewhere to sit down, because some of the part-timers, just a few, have nothing but a large tarmac area and no inside facilities whatsoever. It's a grim thought, particularly in the middle of winter.

The course should start with the instructor checking your documents. He will look at your licence and make sure that it's not only current but that you also have motorcycle entitlement on it. If you've brought your own bike along he will check that you have insurance and also a current MOT if one is needed. And he should also look to make sure that you've got a valid tax disc on the bike, as well as correctly displayed L-plates.

Some ATBs 'give you something'. At my place we're fairly generous – you get a big fat envelope filled with all sorts of wonders. A good part of it is road safety leaflets on topics like drink driving, tyres, clothing, and even tram signs as this is Manchester and we are environmentally ahead of the rest of the country. Of more interest is a magazine, discount vouchers redeemable at local bike shops, course notes, and a motorcycle test application form. I don't understand ATBs that don't give these out. They're no longer available at the Post Office and as a result, they're not that easy to get hold of. If you do attend one of these backward places then pay a visit to your nearest test centre – it doesn't have to be somewhere that does bike tests, and pick one up in the waiting room where there should be a large pile.

Your instructor will then talk to you about a number of topics, including:

THE AIMS OF THE COMPULSORY BASIC TRAINING COURSE

Bit of an airy fairy job this. You're there to learn to ride a bike aren't you, so presumably it's got something to do with that. The course will assume everyone is a novice, even if you have had some previous experience, and you will be gradually introduced to the wonders of motorcycling in a patient and steady manner. Things should be taken at your own pace and you shouldn't be rushed into doing anything that you're not ready for. Besides training you to ride and control a motorbike, the course will also prepare you for going out on to the road by teaching you how to use the brakes properly, how to move off correctly, and how to do left and right turns and emergency stops. You will cover other features like roundabouts, traffic lights, crossings, and so on. In other words, the basics of riding a bike and surviving on the roads.

LEGAL REQUIREMENTS FOR RIDING ON THE ROADS

When riding on the road on your own machine, you need to have insurance, road tax (unless the machine is more than 25 years old), and, if necessary, an MOT. The bike must also be roadworthy, which is not the same as having a current MOT certificate. If it's your own bike, you should also have a log book. If you're riding a so-called grey import, make sure it complies with UK specification, although it has to be said that the feedback that is coming through from the insurance companies these days seems to indicate that not as much importance is placed on this subject as there used to be.

WHY MOTORCYCLISTS ARE MORE VULNERABLE THAN MOST ROAD USERS

I used to think this was a really stupid point to include in the CBT course as it was so obvious, or at least so it seemed to me. My experience of teaching CBT says otherwise. It's amazing how people hum and ha when you ask them this question. And the answer is: because motorcyclists don't have a big metal box around them to offer protection. In fairness it goes a shade deeper than that. Car drivers don't always appreciate the problems bikers have. They aren't ready for the fact that when a rider comes to a sharp bend he has, initially, to slow down – more than a car will have to do. They don't make allowances for the effect high winds can have on motorcycle stability. In short, motorcyclists are more vulnerable than other road users because they take up less space, are less visible and fewer in number than other road users.

THE IMPORTANCE OF HAVING THE RIGHT EQUIPMENT AND CLOTHING

Oh, a dearly beloved subject of mine and one I'll go on about in detail on pages 42–52. When you climb on a motorbike, you should be dressed accordingly. You might not care, but your wife, children, girlfriend, boyfriend, husband, or dog might.

In talking on this subject though, one is always very conscious of the restrictions placed on people by money, or rather a lack of it. The response you'll get from me is do the best you can. If you have an overall budget with which to buy everything, spend more on correct clothing and maybe even less on the bike. If you have a budget then I hope there is something in there for clothing. There is, isn't there? Good.

THE IMPORTANCE OF READING AND UNDERSTANDING THE HIGHWAY CODE

There are no ifs or buts. Read it, know it. Do so while you're training so that if there is something in it that you don't understand, you can ask Mr. Instructor. No one's saying you should know it off by heart, but at the very least you should be very familiar with it, even intimately acquainted with it if you're lonely and have no social life. It's a credit to the Department of Transport who publish it because the current version is easy to read and nearly, almost, enjoyable.

THE NEED TO MATCH SPEED TO ROAD AND TRAFFIC CONDITIONS

Essentially what this means is, if you are in heavy traffic that is crawling along at 20 mph., then don't try and drive at 40. If it's pouring with rain or is snowy or icy or foggy then slow down accordingly. Even the densest trainee has enough common-sense and a genuine interest in self-preservation to ride instinctively at broadly the speed appropriate to the prevailing conditions. At this point on the course, your instructor will grab you by the ear and drag you outside, if you're not outside already. He should then give you an eyesight check by asking you to read a vehicle number plate from just over 20 metres away. I will deal later with the penalties of failing this part on your test. If you fail here too, then your instructor should tell you to go away and visit an optician. Remember that the CBT course includes a ride on the road and if you can't see clearly where you're going, then there isn't much point. If you do wear glasses then remember to bring them.

THE MOTORCYCLE

If you're hiring a machine from the training school then it's usually at this point that you get introduced to it. You will want it to be friendly and helpful because you're very probably going to abuse it and maybe even hurt it. It will be sympathetic and understanding because that's its job, but if it doesn't take to you and your affair becomes a battle of wills, then you will probably lose.

ATBs use a variety of different machines, but among the most popular is the Honda CG125. It is a durable four-stroke with tremendous economy, easily maintained and with broad appeal. You might find yourself on a two-stroke, probably a 100 cc machine, belching out large clouds of smelly blue smoke every time you get going. Some trainers are even offering the Kawasaki KMX 125, a trail-style machine designed to attract younger people.

The basic controls on any modern machine are identical, no matter what model. There will certainly be subtle differences in the location of the odd switch – the fuel tap or the choke for example – but it should be possible to climb from one machine to another without too many problems.

CONTROLS AND INSTRUMENTS

KICK-START

No use moaning about this. It's unlikely you'll have an electric start (unless you happen to be on a moped or scooter) and you won't get one until you get a grown-up bike. Electric starts involve the complicated process of pressing a button momentarily to start the engine. The kick-start means you have to pull a lever out from the side of the bike and kick down on it with the underside of your right foot in a sharp and forceful manner. The degree of force needed does vary from model to model and while with some bikes you need a fair bit of oomph, with others virtually no exertion is required. Gently place your foot on the rubber rung on the kick-start, which is always on the right side of the bike, at the point where it naturally rests when pulled out from the side of the machine, and then swing down from that position, following it through all the way down. Don't necessarily expect the bike to fire first time. As soon as you've kicked, remove your foot from the lever immediately because if you don't, you will hear the most awful crunching noise. One very important point: as soon as the engine is going, push the kick-start back into its resting place. This should be something that you learn to do instinctively. It is potentially dangerous to ride off with it still out. With one or two machines, in order to use the kick-start, you need to push up the right side foot-peg first.

THROTTLE

The throttle is always located at the end of the **right** handlebar. Twist it towards you and the bike goes faster. Release it and the bike begins to slow down. The throttle is spring

loaded and if you release it, it returns to the closed position. When you're starting a bike, it is usual to twist the throttle a little bit while you simultaneously kick it over.

CLUTCH

The clutch lever is always on the **left** handlebar. You pull this in immediately prior to changing gear and then slowly release it afterwards. Clutch control is a vital part of learning to ride a bike. For example, sometimes you will need to ride very slowly, possibly even at less than walking pace. If you move along with the bike in gear at that sort of speed, then the chances are that you will need to slip the clutch, otherwise the engine will stall. Slipping the clutch means just easing it slowly under and over the biting point. And before you ask, the biting point is the point at which, as you are slowly releasing the clutch, it starts to take effect. You will usually find that you will be able to let the clutch lever out quite a bit before anything starts to happen. While you are finding your feet on a bike and getting used to it, it is vital to remember when moving off in first gear to let the clutch out slowly and in a controlled manner. Never change gear without using the clutch.

FRONT BRAKE LEVER

This is always located on the **right** handlebar. There are two brakes on a motorbike. Of the two, this is the more important. Pull it in towards you with your right hand and the bike slows.

REAR BRAKE PEDAL

This is located in front of and slightly below the level of the **right** footrest. Tread carefully on this with your right foot and the bike slows. When you apply any brake, collectively or individually, the rear brake light will come on.

INDICATOR SWITCH

There are a number of different types, however all operate the indicator flashers. Switches can vary in shape from a rocker switch to a sliding button. Turn it to the left and, as if by magic, the left indicators will come on. Warning: indicators on most motorcycles are **not** self-cancelling. When you have completed a turn, you must remember to turn the thing off yourself. Leave it on inadvertently and following traffic will presume you're going to take that next left or right turn and will position itself accordingly. This could have serious and potentially dangerous implications for you, so remember to turn it off. Incidentally, however good you are, you will sooner or later forget – it happens to us all. When you realise, you feel a right prat. It is important to train yourself very quickly to be able to turn the thing on and off without looking down to see what you're doing. This is a very common fault among trainees and, as you have to take your eyes off the road often enough as it is, doing so unnecessarily is to be avoided. If you forget to turn your indicators off on your test, you will probably be failed. One examiner I know gives you one warning, but if it occurs again then it's curtains. Another one takes a view on each situation, so you could be failed on the first occasion or get away with it twice. You've been warned!

HORN

Press the button – usually sited on the **left** handlebar – and it goes 'Beeeeeeeeeep'. A very, very vital tool for a motorcyclist, but for trainees, its use is beset by two problems. The first is, that no matter how emphatically you stress its importance to people, many are still very reluctant to press that button because they consider it an aggressive act.

I should state now that there is a correct and an incorrect use of the horn. Put simply, it is there for you to let other road users or pedestrians know of your presence. An incorrect use of the horn might be to have a blast at some car driver who's just cut you up. Never ever use it in a menacing or aggressive manner.

Correct use of the horn might be, for example, to have a blast to alert a car driver who is moving straight at you into your lane. And although I use the word 'blast', believe you me it is possible to vary the use of the horn so that it can also sound friendly. For example, two medium sized beeps sound nicer than one long one.

The biker needs to learn to develop a thick skin. The fact that the pedestrian/car driver has seen you as a result of you hooting is far more important than whatever reaction your beeping may draw from them.

The other problem with trainees using the horn appropriately is that more often than not, using it correctly in response to a particular situation requires a reaction measurable in milliseconds. One second later and it looks and sounds wrong. The difficulty is that, as with indicators, most learners can't find the horn button without looking down, let alone press it within that fraction of a second. So the answer is practice; get that left thumb used to where it should be going without taking your eyes off the road. To sum up: use the horn sparingly, swiftly and only for the right reasons.

GEAR LEVER

The gear lever is situated slightly above and in front of the **left** footrest. It is used to change gear. Most bikes have five or six gears but some of the East European and Chinese models have only four.

Gears are one of the things that worry and puzzle people before they start training – car drivers in particular are often unduly concerned – but they're really quite simple. What is involved is moving the gear lever either up or down. To move it down, use the sole of your left boot. For up, use the top of your boot, over the toes. First gear is as far down as the lever will go and is the gear you use to move off. If you then ease it gently up, the gearbox will go into neutral – in other words, you are not in any gear at all. If you had moved it a bit more sharpish up from first, it would go straight past neutral into second. It's up again into third, fourth, and fifth etc. as your speed increases.

You change gear according to the speed at which you are travelling. The faster you go, the higher the gear. I can hear you saying, 'But what gear should I be in for what speed?' Well, some speedos do have little displays on them advising you of the maximum speed per gear, but my advice would be to ignore them. What you have to do quite quickly is develop an empathy with the engine. It will tell you what gear to be in by the noise it's making. If it sounds like it's bursting at the

seams and liable to explode within a second, then change into a higher gear. If the bike is leaping a bit or it sounds like it's straining and not having an easy time of it, then change into a lower gear. This empathy and feel is important because unlike a car, you cannot see what gear you're in.

Just as you change up as you go faster, so you change down if the speed of the bike has to drop. Always try to be in the gear appropriate to your speed.

Always remember the golden rule: every time you change gear, whether it be up or down, the clutch should be pulled in first, just prior to the gear change, and then released immediately after.

At the same time as you pull in the clutch, you should also close the throttle. If you don't, nothing major happens, it's just that the engine will continue to rev and the noise could startle you. The bike might not like it much either. As you release the clutch after the gear change, so you should reapply the throttle.

If you think about it, it all seems quite complicated because you're being asked to do three things virtually simultaneously. Can your brain cope? You've got to close the throttle, pull in the clutch, and get your left foot to move the gear lever.

Of course, if you've got a moped or a scooter, then there's a high probability that you've got an automatic gearbox and all you need to do is twist the throttle to make it go and apply the brakes to make it stop. Some clever little chap in Japan did something to that area underneath the seat that does away with all that messing about with clutches and things.

Life can get complicated. There are things called false neutrals. This happens when you're not in proper neutral, but you're not in a proper gear either. Finding false neutrals happens to all motorcyclists and isn't something you should worry about unduly.

MIRRORS

Usually round things sprouting from the right and left handlebars which you look into on a regular basis to see what's going on behind you. Keep them clean. When you are stationary and the engine is turned off, it is permissible to look into them for the purpose of applying make-up or the extraction of nasal hair.

FUEL TAP

The fuel tap regulates the flow of fuel from the petrol tank to the carburettors. It will usually be at the bottom of the petrol tank. As you look at this tap or switch you should just be able to make out, on the edge of it, the words 'On', 'Off', and 'Res'. In order for the bike to be able to go, it needs a supply of petrol to the engine. When the bike is running, the tap needs to be pointing to the 'On' position. When you park, in order to prevent the possibility of fuel leaking from the carburettor, it should be moved to the 'Off' position. It would be interesting to ask the breakdown services how many times they've been called out to a broken down bike only to find that it's not really broken down and that the only problem has been that the clown who calls himself a motorcyclist has forgotten that he turned the fuel tap to 'Off'. So please do remember to move it back to 'On' when you want to get going again.

The 'Res' position means reserve, i.e. your reserve fuel supply. We'll get on to the instrument panel of the bike in a moment or two, but when you look at it you may notice there isn't a fuel gauge. Consequently, you don't know how much petrol you do or don't have left in the tank. As you have a reserve supply, it doesn't really matter. When your bike starts to run out of petrol - all too often at the most inconvenient moment - you simply reach down and spin the fuel tap 180 degrees to the 'Res' position and your back-up supply comes straight in. The amount you have varies from bike to bike, but on the Honda CGs which my school uses you will get a further 50 miles or thereabouts. Remember, when you go on to reserve, you need to fill up soonish. When you have done so, make sure you move the tap back to 'On' because if you don't, the next time you run out of fuel, you will have no reserve fuel to fall back on. And a right lemon you'll feel then!

CHOKE

Helps when starting a cold engine by allowing a higher proportion of petrol into the carburettor. In fact that's a bit of an understatement as a lot of bikes won't start at all when cold, without help from the choke. A choke can be either a lever, as on the Honda CG, or a knob that you pull, and there'll usually be two positions on it – fully open and half open, besides the closed or 'Off' position. The trick is to get the choke back to 'Off' as soon as you can after the engine has started. Riding on choke when the engine is warm and doesn't need it can be harmful. However, if you push it back in too soon, then you run the risk of the bike stalling or hopping around kangaroo style. You need to learn the wiles and idiosyncrasies of your machine as soon as you can.

Incidentally, if the choke on your own bike is not on the facia or around the handlebar area, but instead under the engine on the side of the bike, then my advice is not to ride off with the choke out but wait until the machine has warmed up fully before setting off. You are only going to want to push it back in after a few hundred yards and imagine leaning over and down on your left side trying to find it with your left hand as you're moving along …

LIGHTS SWITCHES

There are two main switches for controlling the lights. The first will work the sidelights and the dipped main beam, and the second, the full main beam. I mentioned sidelights but in fact there aren't any as such. On a bike you have just one headlamp at the front, on the side of which are the two indicator lights, and one red light at the rear, which also doubles as a brake light and is also flanked by two indicator lights. The sidelights I referred to are usually illustrated on the light switch with the letter 'P'. When the switch is in this position, the headlight comes on but with a very low level of brightness. If you wanted to leave a light on when you were parked up while popping into a shop on a winter's evening for a second or two, then the 'P' light would be ideal. Unfortunately however on some machines, you cannot do this without leaving the keys in the ignition and the engine on. Pretty pointless. However an increasing number of bikes have a set position on the ignition switch where, if you move the key to it, the engine stops and you can extract the key from the ignition and the 'P' light comes on.

Every time you turn any light on, the rear red light illuminates as well. When you've got your headlamp on full, a blue

warning light should show up on your dash. You should do all the sensible things with your lights like wash them and replace bulbs when they go.

LEFT HANDLEBAR GRIP

That's just what it is. It does nothing else. You grip it with your hand.

THE BIT WITH ALL THE DIALS ON IT

Call it the dash or facia or whatever else takes your fancy. These can vary from bike to bike and some will have more gizmos on them than others. You will definitely have a speedometer. It will tell you how fast you are going. Near the bottom part of the speedo will be a milometer which records the number of miles the bike has done. If you are moderately mentally dextrous, than this can be useful for reminding you when it's time to fill up with fuel. You'll need to know what you get from a tankful, say 200 miles, and then just make a mental note of what the mileage reading is when you next put petrol in. Then 200 miles later it'll be time to refuel.

You might have a rev counter. This tells you how many somersaults the engine performs every minute. There'll be a red bit at one end, possibly preceded by a dash of yellow, and if you ever see the needle on the rev counter in that area then you are probably doing something very naughty indeed.

There will be a neutral light, a nice shade of green, and it comes on, or should do, when the bike is not in gear – that space between first and second. You will only see it when the ignition is turned on, in other words it doesn't stay on

when you've taken the key out. The light should always be on when the bike is started.

You will have an amber indicator warning light or ideally two of them. They are there to remind you that your indicators are on. When you switch on the directional indicator, the light or lights on the dash will blink. If you have two then the left one will blink when your left one is on and the right one will do the same when the right indicator is in operation. If you've only got the one, then only one light can flash, can't it? Don't whinge or moan. You'll just have to make do. Look down at the dash regularly. You'll be looking at your speedo to check that you're not breaking the law and also checking for a flashing amber light to tell you that you're a moron and have forgotten to cancel your signal.

THE IGNITION SWITCH

The key goes in it and when you turn it on the neutral light comes on (because you will have turned the engine off the previous time making sure the machine is not in gear) and then you can start up. It's not unknown incidentally for people to heave away at the kick-start for ages without anything happening and the bike not firing, only to receive a sharp clout around the helmet from the instructor for having forgotten to turn the ignition on in the first place.

ENGINE

Magnificent beast that it is, it nevertheless looks like it couldn't shift a lawn-mower, let alone your 15 stone bulk. But a fine sturdy lump of cast metal it is and it develops 12 bhp whatever that is when it's at home. That power output is the maximum for a 125 cc that is legal for learners to use. Note though, that in January 1997 the power output allowed increases to 14.6 bhp.

You can go over to the Continent and see the same bikes whizzing around a lot faster than they do here. It is only legal to tinker with restricted machines in an attempt to derestrict them you have passed your test and informed your insurance company and the DVLC in Swansea

THE REST OF THE BIKE

DRIVE CHAIN

Most motorcycles use a chain to drive the rear wheel. Sometimes it can be surrounded by a chain guard. I have to warn the more fastidious among you that when even just talking about the chain, let alone actually doing anything to it, you are inevitably going to get dirty, greasy, messy fingers. There's no way round this I'm afraid. You could, arguably, get someone else to fiddle with it for you and let them get the mess on their own hands, but that's not really right, is it? After all, it is your bike.

The reason that you will get grease on your digits in the first place is that you have to touch the chain in order to check it for tension. You push your finger through the hole in the guard, place it under the chain, and move it up and down. If on the bike you have the underside of the chain is exposed, place your finger midway along. There should be some free play, usually about 20 mm. Your handbook will tell you exactly how much, but if it's too free and easy then it needs tightening.

There are two screws on each side of the rear wheel, near the bottom end of the rear suspension swinging arm (again your handbook will be more specific) which turn for adjustment. Turning the smaller of the two nuts on each side of the wheel will pull it gently back tightening the chain. However, don't go overboard. Move each screw identically, or the wheel will be out of alignment. Too tight a chain is just as much a liability as one that's too slack. If it is too tight, it can snap more easily, leaving you with no drive. Adjust it as close to the handbook measurement as possible.

There's something else that you need to do to the chain – lubricate it. Aerosol cans of chain lube are available from any bike dealer for £1.50 to £3. When you get home, give it a very good shake, put the bike on its centre stand, point the nozzle at the chain through the black bung hole or wherever you have a clear line of sight of the chain, and spray. As you spray, slowly rotate the back wheel so that the chain goes round, giving a nice all-over distribution of the horrible mucus that spurts from the can. It is advisable to keep this can in the garage or just generally near the bike where there is no chance of mixing it up with your favourite intimate deodorant. How often should you do this? Your handbook will tell you. It depends how often you ride but about once a week is a fairly safe bet.

OTHER MUCKY BUSINESS

Oil. Yuk. You will need to check the sump oil in your bike in the same way that you would do in a car. On some bikes you use a dip stick. Unscrew it, pull it out and wipe it off, put it back in and pull it out again. Look at the mark the oil has left on the stick. There'll be a maximum and minimum measure on it and you fill up accordingly.

Some bikes have little windows at the base of the engine which are usually inaccessible and require you to kneel down on the ground and get yourself dirty. You run your engine for two or three minutes and then let everything re-settle for a few moments. You then peer at this little window and can see your oil level that way.

If you have a two-stroke engine machine, do not get the two-stroke oil that mixes with the petrol confused with the sump oil.

TYRES

It is important to make sure tyres are kept at the correct pressures. You don't need to go to a garage every time to do this – just buy yourself a cheap foot pump. You also need to have a good look at them fairly regularly, checking for nails, cuts and general wear. Remember that the tyres are your only contact with the ground. While you can't prevent a puncture that you just pick up while you're riding along, you should certainly be sure that you're not riding around with a slow one. Let me assure you that punctures can be extremely serious for a motorcyclist. Do everything you can to look after your tyres and pay particular attention to tread depth. On a bike, the legal minimum is 1 mm over the centre three quarters width of the tyre. If yours are dodgy, you may not have a particular problem in the dry, but don't count on finishing your journey if it rains.

STANDS

There are two types of motorcycle stand. The *side stand* is a simple 'prop' which sticks out from the side of the machine and literally props it up. The *centre stand* keeps the bike upright and on a more stable footing but is more tricky to operate. It is sometimes called the *main stand*.

It is far safer to park your bike up on the main stand than to leave it on the side stand. It is not unknown for bikes to fall over when on the side stand. Machines can be blown over or just knocked over quite easily, so always park them up on the main stand.

GETTING INTO THE RIGHT "GEAR"

There are a couple of important aspects to clothing. The first is that besides dressing for protection, you also need to consider keeping warm and dry. If you are riding a bike whilst soaked through to the skin or are so cold that parts of you are stiff when you're not sure whether they're meant to be, then your concentration will undoubtedly be affected and your ability to ride safely is at risk. Of course, if the protective riding gear you've bought is also waterproof, then you haven't got a problem on that score, but if it's not, then buy a cheap plastic oversuit that can be scrunched up and packed away for that genuinely rainy day. Be sceptical about claims that an item of clothing is 100 per cent waterproof. In my

experience, sooner or later they always leak and they always leak on the crotch. So, when you take them off after having ridden in the rain, people point and stare at you, clearly suggesting that you've wet yourself. What is the point of putting a product on the market that isn't going to work after a short while? I'm not even entirely convinced that the more you pay for better quality waterproof clothing, then the less chance there'll be of it letting you down.

Oh, by the way, if it's cold, put on extra layers of clothing. Yes, it can be a bind at times being a biker, like spending ten minutes getting ready for a five minute ride, but that's all part and parcel of the fun of being a free-thinking, original, individual member of the human race.

REFLECTIVE GEAR

Make sure you are highly visible – other road users must be able to see you! Why do you think police riders wear those high visibility jackets, those with the yellow background and grey stripes? Because in daylight, the yellow stands out from miles away and at night the grey stripes reflect off car headlights.

I am an absolute fanatic of those reflective jackets and always wear one. They are waterproof and come lined or unlined and will cost between £40 and £60.

They can make you look like a canary and this puts some people off from the fashion point of view. After all, what price your life? Sam Browne belts, presumably named after the old bloke who invented the things, are also effective but less overpowering on the visual senses, if that isn't too much of a contradiction. They too stand out in daylight and reflect at night and are worn round the waist and over the shoulder and cost a pittance.

If you can't be bothered to spend money on reflective clothing, then at least wear something bright to draw attention to your presence on the road. Sad to say, you owe it to yourself to give other road users as little excuse as possible to use their favourite post-accident phrase –'Sorry Mate, I didn't see you!'

THE 'CE' MARK

On July 1 1995 the Personal Protective Equipment directive came into force, a consequence of our membership of the European Community. Its aim was to set out a uniform standard for protective clothing in general, throughout the EU.

On July 1 1995, the Personal Protective Equipment directive came into force, a consequence of our membership of the European Community. It's aim was to set out a uniform standard for protective clothing in general.

What this means for motorcycling equipment is that if they are sold as protective garments, they must carry a CE label (Conformité Européenne). They cannot display this label unless their goods have been laboratory tested under specific conditions.

The problem with this standard is the cost involved, not only of testing, but of subseqently having to bring goods up to the required quality level. Some manufacturers don't do it, and thus these items don't carry the CE label and the garments are described as fashion items. So again, the ball is thrown back into your court. Pay more for better quality or less for inferior.

LEATHER

I don't own a leather suit but it is generally acknowledged that leather offers the best form of protection. In truth there are other materials around these days that claim to do an even better job than leather, claims which I'm not aware of anyone so far disproving, but leather it's always been for bikers and as they're a conservative bunch in some ways, then leather it still often is. Besides, it looks 'hard'. Leather is very good at protecting you against abrasion injuries. Come off your bike and go sliding along a tarmac road for a little while and with the right leather suit on you should get up without too many problems. It can also come with body armour or other suitable protection like 'Protec' which will offer a defence against impact damage too. There are a number of problems though. Firstly, it can be very hot inside a leather suit in summer, even with ventilation holes. In winter it often isn't sufficient on its own to keep you warm, and it's not waterproof, though it will take a light shower. The solution to the latter is to buy the appropriate waxing agent from a bike dealer which is supposed to make a leather suit waterproof, though there are conflicting accounts as to how effective these are. Alternatively, carry a light plastic waterproof suit which can be rolled up into a tiny bundle and stuck somewhere handy, so that it can be retrieved when the heavens open.

For me though there is a far more serious problem with leather than any of the above observations that I've made. It that is, unless you're in the trade or happen to be an expert on the stuff, then you just don't know what you're buying. The problem with it all is that there are just so many different levels of quality. Which animal is it off? Which part of the animal is it off? How's it been treated? What's the quality of the zips on the suit, the stitching on the seams? And so on.

Protective leathers should be made from a hide at least 2 mm thick and, if possible, carry the new European 'CE' quality mark. If it appears that I'm trying to put you off buying leather then let me reassure you that I'm not. What I am suggesting is that, as it's likely to be a major purchase for you, you do as much research as you can before you buy and ask as many questions as you can think of. If there's one thing that holds leather up as the ultimate, it is that the motorcycle racers wear it, and if you're meandering around a track at speeds often approaching 200 mph, you want something that works should you have a little bump.

And that leads on to another point that so far I've just implied. The suits I've just referred to can comfortably cost in excess of £2000. Even at street level you can spend a thousand. Of course, you can get a complete outfit for under £200 but I don't think I'll offer any comment on that.

GORE-TEX

If not leather, what else? Well, there's Gore-Tex, the wonder product of the eighties. I'm sure this must be another of those entities that came about as a result of Man flying off to the moon, like non-stick pans etc... This material can do everything, or so it appears. It's waterproof. In winter it will keep you warm, in summer it will keep you cool. And it's supposed to be even better at protecting you on a tarmac surface than leather. A suit can cost from £500 to £1500 although I have seen suits for under £300. But they don't in all honesty seem that popular and I wonder why that should be? Probably because people feel that if they're going to spend that sort of cash, they might as well go for the extra 'street cred' provided by leather. I mean, some of these Gore-Tex suits make you look like Michelin Man.

I've got one. The reason I bought it was that it could do all those marvellous things and it was an oversuit. I wanted to ride my bike to work and I didn't want to change out of leathers when I got there and then have to put on 'normal' stuff. I'm a lazy, idle slob. So with the Gore-Tex effort I could put on my work clothes first and then slip the suit over it. As to the claims about the material's effectiveness, from my personal experience I found it not brilliant, but adequate.

WAXED COTTON

Moving on, you can buy waxed cotton or nylon riding gear as well. The particular advantage with this sort of stuff is that although it's designed for motorcycling, it can also be used for other outdoor pursuits as well. Nylon in particular has some abrasion resistance properties but it won't be as good as leather. However, this style of clothing is more user-friendly with pockets galore, removable linings, and concealed hoods. And it's usually fully waterproof.

DENIM

To my mind, denim is a waste of time. Having said that, there are a couple of firms that make denim jeans specifically for bikers. These garments have Protec padding on the knees and hips, with reinforced stitching and a double thickness backside. If you must wear jeans, then these are ideal and I must admit that I have a bit of a soft spot for them.

GLOVES

A good pair of gloves is essential. If you know what bike you're getting or have already got, then make a note of what fairing it has, if any. Does it offer any protection to

your hands by way of deflecting the airstream? If not, then you'll need a thicker pair as your hands are going to get colder more rapidly. Again there are varying qualities and once more leather will probably be the best but may not be waterproof. You can get round that by buying waterproof overmitts. You have to watch for things like the quality of stitching and whether it's concealed or if it's exposed and is going to cause the gloves to shred the moment they come into contact with the ground. The metal studs that you sometimes see on motorcycling gloves are excellent. They act as a barrier between the ground and the glove itself so reducing the chances of the gloves being ripped apart.

Obviously gloves should fit well but you will also be looking to retain some 'feel' on the handlebars. A possible way round this is to buy a pair of medium weight gloves for all year round use but supplement it during winter with a pair of woollen ones worn underneath. Some gloves have a pad or even a plastic ridge on the thumb of the right hand. This is so you can wipe the exterior of your visor while you are riding if it's raining.

BOOTS

On the question of biking footwear, there seems to be as many do's as there are don't's. Don't wear trainers. How long do you think they'll last in a scrape? If you're wearing shoes, don't leave laces dangling. In fact, you shouldn't really wear shoes, you should have boots. They haven't particularly got to be riding boots and a good sturdy pair of Doc Martins will probably do the trick. But you do want ankle support and ideally calf protection too. You should get something that's going to feel comfortable when you're walking around as well as when sitting on a bike. Bear in mind as well

that you'll probably wear different thicknesses of socks at different times of the year.

As you might imagine, along with everything else I've written about or will write about on the subject of clothing, there's an enormous selection of biking footwear. Some boots you can slip on and do up in a jiffy, others take an age. Some need regular care, others less so. It's cop-out time from me when I say, 'The choice is yours'. As long as they keep your feet warm and dry and offer genuine protection, they'll do.

I've only really scraped the surface on the subject of clothing and I would advise you to take a mature and sensible approach to it when the moment comes for you to address this question. Your life could depend on it.

SAFETY HELMETS

Every motorcyclist must wear an approved crash helmet when riding on the road. Make sure your training school lends them out and if they do, then I would suggest that you don't buy one before your course starts, but instead wait till you've heard what your instructor has to say on the subject. Hopefully it will be even more informative than I'm going to be and will give you a clearer picture of what you should be looking for before you buy.

If you were to cut a helmet in half, what you would see between the outer shell and the lining inside the helmet where the top of your head rests would be a load of polystyrene. It is this substance that stops your brains getting addled if you have an accident. Imagine whacking a punch-bag and it's the same sort of principle. The leather outer of the punch-bag gives a bit and goes with the blow. But your

hand stops travelling after a short distance because the impact of your blow has been absorbed by the material inside. The same theory works with helmets but in this case the polystyrene does not return to its original shape after a serious bang. You may look at the outside of your lid after an impact with the ground and barely see a mark but the material underneath is compromised forever and you will never be properly protected again.

So if you have an accident then I regret to say you should throw away the helmet you were wearing and get a new one. Don't drop 'em on the ground for the same reasons. Don't leave them perched on the seat of your bike or over the wing mirrors, where they can easily be blown off or knocked off. Cherish them and put them somewhere safe.

Never buy a second-hand one or even use one that's been given to you. How do you know what's been done to it?

Some basic facts. All helmets must comply with BS 6658 type A or B and have a blue sticker with a kite mark on the side of them. If you're buying a helmet to go racing or off-roading then mention it to the shop assistant because your lid will also need a gold or silver ACU sticker too. If it doesn't have a sticker then don't buy it. Visors must conform to BS 4110 and also be marked either XA, YA, or ZA which are all references to the visor's scratch resistance. It is illegal to sell tinted visors.

Having got that out of the way, the nightmare begins. You walk into a shop and see helmets, all with blue stickers on, costing anything from £30 to over £300. How can this be? If they all comply to the appropriate legislation then presumably they all offer the same level of protection. So why do some cost more than others? Well, there are a number of fac-

tors but basically it comes down to material of manufacture, fashion, and quality of finish.

Polycarbonate helmets are usually the cheapest and can often be identified by a moulding line going from the front of the shell to the rear. These helmets should be replaced after about two years or so depending on how often you ride as they are susceptible to weakening due to sunlight exposure. Most people claim that the shell on one of these is weaker than on lids made from other materials, but there is an accessory shop in Manchester with a polycarbonate helmet that is whisked from under the counter to prove otherwise. It has a dent in it. This dent has been caused by a high velocity bolt gun which has been fired at it from close range. If someone had been wearing it at the time, they might have had a bit of a nasty headache but would otherwise be undamaged.

Glassfibre helmets are said to be stronger but supposedly better still are tri-compound lids which are made of a mixture of Kelvar, carbon fibre and poly something or other.

Most modern helmets are full-face style – i.e. they enclose the face and offer chin protection. However traditional open face helmets which comply with the latest standards but offer no facial protection, are still available if you prefer. To my mind the full-face helmet is a much more satisfactory option.

Most helmets fasten with straps underneath your chin These are secured with 'D' ring fasteners. You have to thread the strap through one and then the other. This is a very common means of securing a helmet and also a very primeval one. It can take new riders quite some time to get the hang of it as you are working with your fingers – often in gloves – and can't see what you're doing. I consider it an inbuilt mode of inverted snobbery – experienced riders fasten their helmets

up instantly while gloating at the novice who might struggle for a couple of minutes, and you can get the impression it's a form of mini apprenticeship and that you've not really arrived as a biker until you've mastered the whole stupid system. Some of us are more practically minded and prefer the quick release catches which are a doddle.

But by far the most important point about a helmet is the fit. In short, it should be snug but not tight. You can broadly forget size labels, as one manufacturer's idea of a 60 cm fit is another manufacturer's 64.

It's simply a matter of trying various helmets on until you find the one that fits. And you know it fits because:

With the strap undone and you shaking your head, the helmet doesn't move

With the strap done up and a friend trying to pull it off your head, again it barely moves

Your friend can't pull the thing off your head by pushing it forward from the back of the neck. Please remember that your friend is doing his best to ensure your long term safety and you should not become annoyed with him because he is hurting you. Please be aware that if you start fighting you are likely to be ejected from the shop

There is not too much pressure on the forehead

The cheek pads are snug

I know I've gone over the ground more than once, but I can't stress enough how important it is to wear the right gear. Your life could depend on it, remember!

FIRST RIDE

Everyone will be eager to get aboard the bike for the first time, but there are a couple of things to be dealt with first.

CONTROLLING THE BEAST

TAKING THE BIKE OFF THE MAIN STAND

There it sits, proudly sublime and yet beckoning, waiting for someone to approach so that it can reveal its mechanical charms. DO NOT sit astride the machine, pushing your eager loins forward until the bike rolls off its stand. Three months later you will be back in the bike dealer's getting hold of a new stand because the original one is now warped.

To do the job properly, you stand to the left of the bike with your left foot placed in front and your right foot behind the main stand. That means a slight sideways-on stance. Reach forward and place both hands on the handlebars. The left hand should be clasped around the grip on the left bar but the fingers of the right hand should be over the front brake lever. You do this because if you were to lose control of the bike as it came off the stand, you'd then be able to restrain it by applying the front brake. When you are ready, push forward and the bike will roll off its stand. Make sure you have not got the front brake on when you do this – your fingers should simply be resting on the lever. As it is in the process of coming off the stand, lean it slightly towards you. This will balance the bike correctly and give you control.

Taking the bike off the stand

PUTTING IT BACK ON ITS STAND

To put the bike back on to the stand, again place yourself to the left of the machine. Take hold of the left handlebar with your left hand and with your right foot bring the main stand down from its tucked-away position so that it is resting on the ground. The stand has two legs – the two points that make contact with the ground – and you need to balance the bike so that both its legs are touching the floor. One of its legs is under your right foot but the other one is further away under the bike and you can't see it from where you're standing. If you gently push the bike away from you or pull it towards you, you will feel the moment when both legs are making contact with the ground.

Place your right hand at a suitable point under your side of the seat, preferably on the metal frame. Lift here, and pull back, and at the same time press down with your right foot. The bike should go up easily on to the main stand. Try and avoid pulling on the left handlebar although you may find yourself doing so. The reason for holding this bar is supposedly for one of balance only but until you have mastered the technique correctly, you may find that your main source of leverage comes from here.

Women in particular can experience difficulty getting this exercise right as it certainly does involve an element of strength, but it's as much a knack as anything else. And to be honest, I find it impossible to explain this 'knack'. All I can

Putting the bike back on the stand

say to those that struggle is that they will manage it eventually and they always do. I then ask how they've done it and the can't tell me.

GOING FOR A STROLL

You'll be asked next to push the bike around the training area. Why? Not a lot of point if you can go off riding all day without a hitch only to come back home, have to park the bike round the back and trip head over heels while you are doing it. You need to be able to control the machine at walking pace and to cope with the weight. You should be asked to push it to the left and right in a fairly tight circle. As you are walking, the bike will be leaning in towards you and the fingers of the right hand will be placed over the front brake lever.

TIME TO GET GOING

At last you get to climb on the blessed thing. The first thing you need to do is start the engine, so in goes the key and the ignition is turned on. The neutral light appears. It is lazy and bad riding practice to start the bike in gear. The neutral light tells you that you're not in gear, however it can lie to you. To double check, gently roll the machine backwards and forwards, about a metre each way. Assuming that the bike rolls freely, then you are genuinely in neutral. Do not sit down. If the engine is cold, use the choke. Get the kick- start out of its hiding place and twist the throttle slightly towards you while at the same time applying the front brake lever. Kick down hard on the kick-start with your right leg while keeping your balance and weight on your left. With luck the bike will burst into life. If it doesn't, try again.

Each time you use the kick-start, whether the bike fires up or not, take your foot off it straight away. As soon as the engine starts, release the throttle otherwise the engine will scream away and it won't be very happy doing that when cold. Get the choke back in as soon as you can.

I said something in the last but one paragraph which, if you've been paying attention, should have leapt off the page at you and caused you to mutter, 'What is he playing at?' I said that you should twist the throttle towards you and also apply the front brake lever. If you think about it, I am asking your right hand to go in two different directions at the same time and if you have a small mitt then you might find this a shade difficult. But you will do it anyway because I have told you to. When you are starting a bike, it is important to keep a brake on for two reasons. Firstly, you are in proper control of the machine and it can't roll away if, for example, you happen to be starting up on a hill. Secondly, you will be showing a brake light and that is a signal to other road users that you are not about to shoot off in front of them as they approach.

It has to be the front brake that is held on as your right foot is being used on the kick-start.

The engine is going. Sit down on the bike with both hands on the bars and your right foot up on the back brake. You are now in what's called the *Waiting Position* – the stance you would assume when out on the road if you found yourself stationary for more than a few seconds. The engine is still in neutral which is the third facet of the *Waiting Position*.

PREPARING TO MOVE OFF

The next step is to put it into gear. Your instructor should have been in very close attendance all the while as we are assuming you are a complete novice, getting ready to move off for the first time. Even if you drive a car, you will not necessarily find learning to ride a bike any easier. This idea is commonly-held, but entirely illogical.

You should note that the exercises in this section are designed to ensure that you develop basic skills for starting, moving off and stopping before you are let out on the public road. They should be practised only in the grounds of the training school. Once you venture out on to the road, following the Moving Off procedure described from pages 74–76.

Of course if you've ridden before and are confident that you can manage moving off without any further assistance, then all your instructor has to do is tell you to ride off in a straight line for a few yards and then bring the bike to a stop. If you are a complete beginner and scared to death at this point, then I will tell you what he should do. He should stand astride the front wheel facing you. He should then give the following instructions:

 Apply the front brake

 Pull in the clutch

 Take your right foot off the back brake and put in on the ground

 Bring your left foot up and tap the gear lever firmly downwards so that the bike goes into first gear. The neutral light should go off

Put your left foot back down on the ground and bring the right foot back up and on to the back brake

Then, and only then, release the front brake and resume a proper grip on the throttle

This method of putting the bike into gear is known as the Hendon Dance, named after the police driving school at Hendon where this system was first applied. The principal detail to point out is that while you were going through the actions of putting the bike into first gear, you had a brake on. There was no gap in brake continuity. You were fully in control of your machine all the time.

As you pulled the clutch in, your instructor's right hand should have been placed over your left hand, so ensuring that you did not release the clutch accidentally. Not that he doesn't trust you but he should also place his left hand over yours on the front brake lever, after you've popped it into gear, as a further precaution. Remember, he's still standing facing you.

What he is doing in fact is making sure that he is in full control of the situation and demonstrating that your safety is the paramount consideration. He may well ask you next to wind the revs up a little via the throttle and to then slowly, very slowly, let the clutch out. His right hand will still be there shadowing your left. You are not going to let it out all the way, just to the biting point. You will see how much travel there is on the clutch lever before anything starts to happen and also what begins to occur when the clutch does bite, namely that the revs drop and the bike tries to edge forward.

Your instructor will not let you set off yet though, not until you're happy to give it a try. You can practise partially releasing the clutch a few times to get settled down, but you can't put the big moment off any longer. You are worried. You think you're going to go shooting off into the stratosphere, the bike will do a wheelie, or everybody else will just collapse laughing at your feeble attempts at riding. All these things could happen, but they won't if your instructor is doing his job properly. He should now step back from the bike about five or six paces, still facing you. Remember you are still in gear.

At this point it's just a question of doing what you were doing before, although the instructor's hands will not be covering yours. This time you continue to release the clutch slowly till the bike starts to edge forward. As it does, clear the back brake with your right foot and bring your left foot up on to the peg.

You are riding towards the instructor. He has the option of stopping you if he wants simply by outstretching his arms and leaning in towards you as you loom up large. His hands will be guided towards the clutch and front brake and as you 'hit' him, his hands close on those levers and you come to a stop virtually immediately. Remember he's only been standing a short distance in front of you and there will be very little momentum. Alternatively, if he's happy with what he's seen, he can stand aside as you approach and let you carry on in your own sweet way. *Voilà!* You're riding a motorcycle!

But you may not be. You may have stalled it. It's a common fault among learners and the principal reasons are a lack of revs and too fast a release of the clutch.

Your instructor will have told you to wind the revs up, but some people are a bit frightened of the noise and are convinced that they will lose control the moment they try to get going. Well, you will do if you just let go of the clutch but the engine can be screaming its head off and you can still be in perfect control as long as you don't lose your head and continue to release that clutch slowly. And that means you're still releasing it slowly even when you are moving. All the way till it's completely out.

When you are moving and want to stop, all you have to do is close the throttle, pull in the clutch, and gently apply a brake. In their panic, some people forget to close the throttle but it doesn't really matter. Even forgetting to put a brake on isn't really that important providing you're not about to hit something. What does matter is the clutch because as soon as that's pulled in the bike starts to slow. If you do forget about the throttle then don't be distracted by the continuing noise. Just concentrate on stopping. Again, if your instructor has been doing his job, he will have been running along side of you while you've been moving. He will call out instructions like, 'Pull this, push that!' and so on.

Hopefully, he will get you to practise moving off quite a few times so that you begin to feel more at ease doing it. Your aim should be to speed the process up but take it slowly at first. Frequent moving-offs require frequent stops and these too should become smoother and neater.

You ride round the perimeter of the training area for a while, getting used to the sensation and just generally settling down. Eventually you'll be stopped and the instructor will then ask you to ride off again but this time you'll be expected to

change gear. It sounds complicated because you're required to do three things at virtually the same time:

 Set off in first

 When you're ready, close the throttle, pull in the clutch, and move the gear lever up sharpish with your left foot so that it goes from first to second gear, passing through neutral

 Re-apply the throttle and smoothly let the clutch out again.

You will probably only be asked to go up and down between first and second at this stage as your training area will most likely not be large enough to sustain further higher gear changes. Some places do have very large sites and if you do find yourself on one then consider yourself fortunate.

When you change down from second to first, you'll need initially to slow the bike down because if you're going too fast when you let the clutch back out in first gear you may well lock the back wheel up. Nasty noise, long tyre mark, bit of a smell, grumpy instructor, but other than that nothing else to worry about. If you do lock it, it's extremely unlikely you'll fall off.

Remember: you change gear, both up and down, according to the speed you're travelling at.

What do you do if you're frightened at the idea of moving off by yourself for the first time and the instructor isn't shadowing you or standing over you but instead is well out of the way and is just giving verbal directions? Either shrug your

shoulders, bite your bottom lip, concentrate hard and be brave and give it a go, or insist he comes and stands a lot nearer to you. Don't be afraid to speak up. Explain that you're not very confident and need more assistance. You may think you're making a fool of yourself or causing an unnecessary fuss but so what? You've paid your money for the course and are entitled to be treated with consideration. And to be taught in a safe manner. If you're seriously unhappy then climb off and cause a scene.

SLALOM

This is an exercise that used to feature in the old Part One Test but is not compulsory in CBT. However many ATBs still utilise it as it is a good way of beginning to develop clutch/throttle/ brake control.

You are looking at a line of cones, perhaps five or six, spaced about 1.75 metres apart. You have to ride through them, weaving your way in and out. The objective is not to miss any or knock any over, and not to stall or put a foot down. Without any direction, most people swing out wildly to get round them and wonder why they miss so many. The trick is to keep your passage through the cones in as straight a line as possible. You must also judge your speed accurately; a too fast and you miss the odd one, too slow and the foot comes down. Some people can just sail through at an even speed without touching anything but most need to use the clutch, back brake, and vary the throttle to make it.

FIGURE OF EIGHT

This exercise can vary as to how precisely it is carried out but we use a largeish box marked out on the training area in the middle of which we place two cones, about 1.5 metres apart. You have to ride through them, carrying on in a straight line to virtually the edge of the box, turn, for example to the right (it doesn't matter whether you go left or right the first time) and just keeping inside the box, follow the perimeter round. When you come to the first corner, turn, when you come to the next one turn again and this time half-way along turn to your right again and go back through the cones. Again go through and out in a straight line almost up to the edge but this time turn to your left and repeat the whole thing in reverse.

The object is to keep within the box, which you may find hard at first, without putting a foot down. It requires the same features of control as in the slalom – utilisation of the throttle, clutch and rear brake. This exercise featured on the old Part 1 and I remember having terrible trouble with it myself. I only just reached an acceptable standard and as I now consider myself to be the best motorcyclist in the UK and clearly an expert, I would say to you 'Don't despair' if you struggle with this at first.

SLOW RIDE

This exercise can be conducted in a number of different ways but essentially what is required of you is to ride along the training area in a straight line as slowly as you can without stalling or putting a foot down. Yet again, the elements of control are the same as those featured in the previous two exercises.

The way we do this at our place is to have an instructor walk beside the rider on the right-hand side of the bike with his left arm extended. The object for the rider is to try and ensure that he keeps the front wheel of the bike under the instructor's arm at all times. I said the instructor will walk beside the rider but that's a bit of a lie. We enjoy torturing trainees at our place so to make it more of a challenge, the instructor will start off walking, then break into a run, then suddenly slow to a virtual standstill, shoot off again, and so on. All the time we are reminding the trainee of what his objective is as it's something that seems to get forgotten quite easily in the struggle to master this exercise.

Slow ride

We never lower our arms under any circumstances so if the instructor breaks out into a run and then suddenly starts walking very slowly and the trainee doesn't respond quickly enough on the brakes, then his head hits the instructor's arm.

One novel way that I've heard of this exercise being conducted is for all the trainees to be lined up and told they're going to have a race, except that the winner is the last person to the finishing post. I regard this method as unsatisfactory as it introduces an element of fun and frivolity into the proceedings and trainees must remember at all times that they are not there to enjoy themselves!

BRAKING

It will come as no great shock to you when I tell you that this is considered to be a fairly important topic. After all, you've been taught how to get moving but it would be a big help if you could stop correctly as well.

There's nothing like repetition so I'll say it again. Different training schools have different ways of explaining and teaching a particular subject. Therefore, don't be surprised if the way that your ATB approaches this is completely different to the way I'm going to go through it.

We start off by warning pupils that we're going to ask a trick question: 'What stops a bike?' 'Well', thinks the trainee, 'the obvious answer is of course the brakes but that clearly can't be the right response because we've been warned it's a trick question'. As an instructor, you stand there watching brains whirring round. You wait while feet are shuffled and heads are turned downwards in apparent concentrated thought. Then suddenly someone says, without really knowing why, 'The clutch'. Someone else says 'The gears' and so it goes on without anyone ever getting near.

We then smugly say, 'Watch this' and take hold of a bike and roll it forward a few feet. The front brake is then applied and the trainees are asked what they saw the bike do.

What they witnessed when the front brake was stuck on was the chassis of the bike pitch forward and down. 'That', says the instructor 'is what stops a bike.' The weight of the machine and the rider being thrown forward on to the front wheel and tyre, and the resulting increased grip with the road surface brings everything to a stop.' So a bright pupil asks, 'How do you set that up?' And the embarrassed instructor says, 'Er, by applying the brakes'.

That's not strictly true. You set that up by applying the front brake. Of the two brakes, when in general use the front brake is the more important of the two and the more powerful. When stopping in a straight line in dry conditions, apply the front brake just fractionally ahead of the rear brake and put about 75 per cent of your braking effort through the front and 25 per cent through the rear. All this is of course approximate, as you have no means of measuring your brake pressure exactly.

All that the brakes do is to slow the rotation of the wheels. Try braking on sheet ice. The wheels will stop going round but the bike will continue on and on and on and on. Without that front tyre grip on the road surface, there is nothing.

When it's wet, you don't want that forward 'throw' on to the front wheel. Instead you want an evenly distributed braking effect so both brakes are applied simultaneously with equal pressure.

Remember what I've written above and apply it. It is the correct way to use the brakes on a motorcycle. If you are a pedal cyclist then you may be a bit wary of trusting the front brake and regarding it as the primary stopping tool. Well, rid your-

self of that attitude and forget about bicycles. You are now on the paramount means of two-wheeled transport.

You will probably be given a demonstration emphasizing the effect of each brake. An instructor might ride across the training area to a fixed point and when he reaches it he will apply the brakes, the first time by using the rear brake only. The spot where the front wheel has come to a stop is marked with a cone. The exercise is repeated twice more, the second time using the front brake only and the third time using both brakes correctly. Each time a cone is placed close to the spot where the front wheel has stopped. When finished you have before you a perfect illustration of the effectiveness of each brake. The rear brake on its own takes the longest distance to stop the machine, the front brake on its own is better, but use both brakes and the advantage is clear to see. This is the correct way to stop a bike.

There are two exceptions to the rule. The first is when you are riding in slow-moving traffic, crawling along through a city centre for example. In traffic like that, where it is stop-go, stop-go, just use the back brake to come to a halt. It gives better control and consequently smoother stopping.

The other exception is when the bike is leaned over. The technical term for this is 'going round a bend'. Of course, being a well-trained rider, whenever you approach a bend you will attempt to judge its severity in advance and adjust your speed accordingly. You will not enter a bend too fast. There is an old saying applied to bends that goes, 'Slow in, fast out'. You are, regretfully, also a human being and as such you are likely to make the occasional mistake. You will be going round a bend and as you do you will say to your-

self, 'Cripes! I am going too fast. If I don't take remedial action promptly, I may well be in serious trouble'. In all probability you may not use those exact words. If you find yourself in that sort of situation then you need to act very quickly but also calmly. Apply just the back brake gently.

If you apply the front brake when going through a bend, there is a strong chance that you might lock the front wheel up. If you do that you are almost certain to come off. Whatever you do, don't panic. One of the major reasons bikers come off on bends is that they've gone in too fast, realised late that they've got it wrong and, in a frenzy, grabbed any lever and pedal to hand. Result? Serious accident.

There is some debate these days as to whether it is still legitimate to preach to trainees that they should never use the front brake while the bike is leant over. There have been advances in both steering and tyre technology which make use of the front brake in these conditions viable. At this stage in your motorcycling career, it is safer to assume those advantages do not apply to your bike.

ROAD SURFACES

Your instructor will also talk to you about road surfaces and the sort of things you need to watch out for. It is important that you are aware of and can recognise hazards on the road which can make braking perilous.

RAIN

Clearly, when it's raining, things aren't so great on two

wheels as when it's dry. Items on the road that are usually no problem suddenly take on a different context when wet.

MANHOLE COVERS

Not a worry in the dry but perilous in the rain. Firstly, if you can, try and avoid them but if you spot them late then it would probably be more dangerous to swerve round them than to ride over them. Remember that even on a small bike you're only likely to have one wheel on the cover at any time. If travelling over one in the rain, don't brake or accelerate.

The problem with manhole covers is doubly compounded by the fact that sewers frequently follow the lie of the road. Blockages in sewers will occur on bends so that is the most popular place to locate these motorcycling hazards. And going round a bend on a bike means leaning it, however slightly, which also means there is less tyre on the road and consequently less grip. Beware of wet manhole covers!

LEAVES

Avoid even when apparently dry and nice and crunchy. Frequently a soggy mess underneath.

LOOSE GRAVEL

Avoid like the plague. Do not brake if at all possible.

DIESEL

A very serious hazard for motorcyclists. In fact so much so that when a spillage is announced on a radio traffic report,

motorcyclists are often targeted as the recipients of the information. The first problem with diesel is that you can't see it. If you have any clue at all as to its presence, other than the sight of other bikers in front of you sliding all over the place, then it will be the smell, but often you only get the whiff when you're right on top of it.

So what do you do? Well you can use your common sense and watch out for it in the more obvious places. Most diesel gets on the road because the lorry driver has overfilled his tank. It then spills out round a sharp corner or a roundabout. Anywhere in fact where heavy wagons, buses, coaches and so on linger and gather is potentially risky.

BLACK BANDING

When 'they' dig a hole in the road and then refill it and blend it back in with the surrounding surface, a black bitumen mush is put down to seal it all off. There is no problem with this stuff when it's dry but it is treacherous when wet. There are laws which state that contractors are supposed to limit its width to no more than five centimetres but I would tactfully suggest that this is not always observed. On a narrow road this can cause other problems like for example where exactly do you place the bike on the road to avoid this mess? If you ride to the right of it you may be taking yourself too close to oncoming traffic. If you ride to the left you may end up in the gutter. Be vigilant and try to adopt the best compromise.

WHITE LINES AND ARROWS

I'm referring here to the white lines down the middle of a road and to the large directional arrows also frequently

painted on to a road surface. Again no problem in the dry but can be a bit iffy in the wet. Zebra crossings are not usually too bad but on the Continent they can be lethal.

CAT'S-EYES

Diabolical in the wet.

TRAM LINES

Because here in Manchester where I live we're such a forward-looking urban community, sensitive to the environment and all that stuff, we have a tram system which other less innovative cities have only just got round to copying. That brings tram lines, sunk into the road, which are not nice to ride over in the wet. Steer well clear.

COLD-PLANING

When a road is being resurfaced, the old tarmac is first lifted off, leaving squiggly grooves. For some reason, contractors seem to like to leave a road like this for some time, perhaps to let it get a good airing, before re-covering it. Motorcycles do not like this kind of surface and it is imperative that you drop your speed considerably when travelling over it. 10 or 15 mph is a safe maximum. Riding on this gives a most peculiar feeling, as if you have no control over your machine any longer. This is because your tyres are inclined to follow the grooves and they are not always straight.

ICE AND SNOW

There are motorcyclists, and I used to be one of them, who take the view that nothing but nothing will keep them off the roads. This group is by far and away the minority within the motorcycling fraternity, many riders being wimps who put their bikes away on August 31 and who don't take them out again till March or April. If you look around when there's ice or snow about, you will see a few people out on bikes but they tend to be the lunatic fringe like dispatch riders or pizza delivery lads. Or me. Well, actually, not any more.

Nothing happened to make me change my mind, no accident or anything like that, it was just that I decided that the holy credo of riding 365 days a year, come what may, just wasn't worth the bravado any more. Call it getting older or just selling out - these are criticisms I cannot refute, much as it hurts me to say so. Certainly I ride all the year round but if there's a sharp winter's feel to the weather, like six foot snow drifts or a frozen River Mersey, then I reluctantly decide that it might be more appropriate to take a different mode of transport. And I suggest that you do the same.

You will have gathered already that as a motorcyclist there is enough for you to do and think about while you are riding to give you a headache just contemplating it all. Well here's something else. Learn to read the road. Learn to watch out for these types of hazards and learn how to deal with them.

GET MOVING

Your instructor has been talking to you about braking for some time. You may well have seen at least one demonstration. Time for you to climb back on the bike. A box formed out of cones is set up through which runs a horizontal line. The idea is to ride along the training area towards the box and bring the machine to a stop with the front wheel bang on the line. To do this, you will have to apply the brakes correctly.

If it helps, equate this exercise with stopping at the thick white line at traffic lights. Of course in that situation you would stop just behind the line.

Trainees make all sorts of mistakes and misjudgements in attempting this exercise. Many are so concerned about being accurate that they pull up ages before the line and then creep along. Would you do that out on the road for real? Try it and see how long it is before you're rear-ended. Focus on where you want to stop and try for a smooth approach and braking effort. The first thing that should happen is that the revs drop. Then the brakes are applied gradually. When you do come to a stop it should be the left foot that touches down on the ground.

Some people forget to pull in the clutch just prior to coming to a halt. Don't. Some pull the clutch in too early with the result that they 'coast'. Dangerous. Some approach the whole thing like an emergency stop and come rushing along and put the brakes on late. Silly.

MOVING OFF

It is at this point that you might well be introduced to a riding system which will encompass the all-important point of rear

observation. Before you move off - in fact before you carry out any manoeuvre – adopt the system we call LSL:

 **Look Behind**

 **Signal and Gear**

 **Lifesaver**

A Look Behind is just what it says: a look over your **right** shoulder, to check what's going on behind you. Don't ever be tempted to use a Look in the Mirror – they all have blind spots.

Signal – with your indicators. There's no need to use arm signals unless your bike is not fitted with indicators. If this is the case, get them fitted, or get rid of the bike.

Lifesaver – this is not the same as the Look Behind. A Lifesaver is a look over your shoulder to check those areas which fall into the blind spots we mentioned. It is always given over the shoulder in the direction in which you are about to turn. So, Left Turn, Left Lifesaver. Moving off, Right Lifesaver. Always remember your Lifesaver. It is the most important action in motorcycling and it could, quite literally, save your life.

Assuming that you want to join the general flow of traffic, then what you do next after the Lifesaver is move off, then cancel your signal. Next, adopt what we call the *riding position*. This isn't a specific reference to the way you sit on the bike but instead is a guide as to where you should place your machine on the road. It is an interesting subject that appears to be causing the DSA some confusion these days.

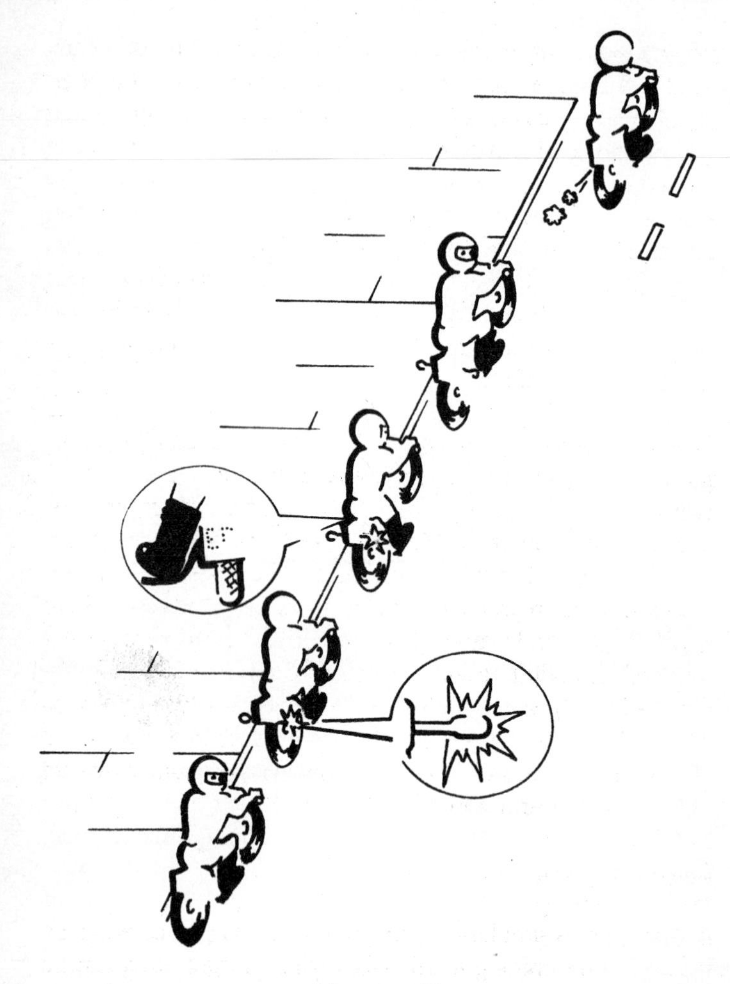

Moving off

It used to be a golden rule that you kept left unless you had a very good reason for moving out, like getting past parked cars or lining yourself up for a right turn. I assume the reason

for this was to it enable following traffic to overtake if they wanted to. It's a load of bunkum. It might well have been practical 20 years ago but it isn't now and they recognise that any motorcyclist worth his salt, the moment his test is out of the way, is going to place himself in the middle of his lane along with the rest of the general flow of traffic so that he can be seen and can himself see more clearly. Police riders are taught to ride extremely defensively. If you carefully analyse what they do, then much of it actually involves blocking the progress of other car drivers so as to render the police rider's situation more safe.

In the motorcycling manual that the DSA publish they now suggest that you keep to the centre of the lane. I would recommend this only when you are on a road with more than one lane going in each direction. Generally, when you have moved off from the side of the road, my suggestion to you is that you position yourself about a metre from the kerb. There is no need to ride along with a tape measure in your left hand, constantly checking that you're maintaining that distance all the time - an approximation will be sufficient. Adopt that position gradually. Don't yank the handlebars sharply to the right. After you've given the final Lifesaver and have set off, be positive and don't dawdle.

LEFT TURNS

It is usual for a simulated road system made up of cones to be set up on the training area so that left and right turns can be explained and practised. Some ATBs have a road layout painted on to their training area which is even better.

A left turn is a simple utilisation of the LSL system. Remember, particularly if you know where you are going,

that it is a good idea to let other road users know of your intentions as soon as is practical. Don't try and keep it all a secret that you can chuckle over and gossip about with your bike. Share it with the other drivers on the road if only so that they know you're up to something and can make allowances for you. Do start your system earlier rather than later.

The procedure is quite simple:

Look Behind

'I'm going to be turning left soon so let's see what's happening behind me.' If the road is clear and it is safe to do so...

Signal

If there's any confusion, then let me confirm it's a left signal because you're turning left. It should come on as soon as you've looked behind. Make sure you do not put your signal on if there's a left turn before the one that you want. Following traffic will presume it's the first left you're going to take. Put it on as you're passing that first turn.

If there are two left turns located very close to each other and it's the second one that you want, then you have to weigh up the disadvantage of putting your signal on early, before the first turn which may be confusing to traffic following you and to vehicles waiting to pull out, or leaving it too late. The answer is......... make your own mind up! Each case will be different and there is no hard and fast rule. Not only that, but as with many motor cycling situations, you'll have to think quickly too. Life's not easy.

Begin to slow down. Use the brakes to drop your speed and come down through the gears. What's the best gear to be in

to go round a turn? It's easy to be flip and say, 'Whichever is the most appropriate' but I know that's no help to you. Usually second gear is the best but it does depend on each bike. It will almost certainly be either first or second. Try for yourself and see how your bike feels.

Lifesaver

It shouldn't be done too early and it shouldn't be done so late that your head is still over your as you make the turn. And over which shoulder is it? Remember, Left Turn, Left Shoulder.

'But', I hear you squawk, 'what am I supposed to be looking for?' Pedal cyclists are one possibility that you might look out for. Other bikers creeping up on your inside is another (don't assume that another biker would never do anything as nasty as that to you). Dogs, pedestrians, anything. Look and check. As you make the turn, make sure that you keep an even course. Do not deviate a little to the right before turning left to 'give yourself a better angle to get round'. Do that and you might find you are on intimate terms with the nearside wing or door of a Ford Sierra that might just be parallel with you at the time. After you've turned, cancel your signal and pick up your speed. *Never coast round with the clutch pulled in.* Keep control of the machine and judge your speed so that you turn comfortably.

Sooner or later when you make a left or a right turn, some moron of a pedestrian will step right out in front of you. What you do depends very much on exactly where they are. Imagine you're half-way into your left turn. Ask yourself this question and answer it very quickly: 'Am I able to complete this turn at the speed I am currently travelling at without caus-

Left Turn Sequence

ing a danger to either the pedestrian or myself?' Only if the answer is a clear and unequivocal 'Yes', then continue. If there's any doubt whatsoever, then stop right where you are, no matter how vulnerable a position that leaves you in. Neither the police nor the authorities in general look kindly on people who run pedestrians over. Even if they're in the wrong, they still have right of way. Of course you can hoot and even shout but if that has no effect, then stop.

RIGHT TURNS

More complicated than lefts as there's more to do Essentially, it is a repetition of the LSL system twice. You are riding along in *the riding position*, about a metre from the kerb and you want to turn right.

 **Look Behind**

 **Signal Right**

 **Lifesaver over the right shoulder**

 **Move to the centre of the road,** just to the left of the white lines

As you cover the first three stages try to keep in as straight a line as possible. If you find you are wobbling all over the place, it is probably because you are turning the whole of the top part of your body around to look behind. Some can do this and remain stable, others can't. If you're the latter, then try keeping your shoulders facing forwards and just turn your head.

The second thing worth mentioning is that you should not move towards the middle of the road until you have given your Lifesaver.

Most importantly, use your common sense about your positioning. I have said that you should place yourself just to the left of the centre white lines. If there is traffic coming towards you then give a little and move slightly more to the left, but check before you do. Don't endanger yourself unnecessarily.

You have just arrived at the middle of the road. This is where the LSL system starts to repeat itself. Look behind again. Why? (Remember it's over the right shoulder.) You are checking for cars that might be overtaking you on the wrong side of the road. That is not an offence provided they haven't crossed a solid white line and are not driving recklessly. I have seen cars do this many times. It is worth looking.

Signal – it's still on from before. Leave it on. Begin to slow down and come down through the gears.

Lifesaver – over the right shoulder

Make the turn, cancel your signal, and pick up speed

But what if you can't turn because there is oncoming traffic? Stop. Then ask yourself, 'Am I going to be here a while?' If you think the answer is 'Yes' then put the bike into the *waiting position*. But be alert and don't go to sleep. Look down the line of oncoming traffic and watch for a gap. If you see one coming up, pop the bike back into gear, give another Lifesaver, and be ready to go in advance as soon as the chance comes up. Think ahead.

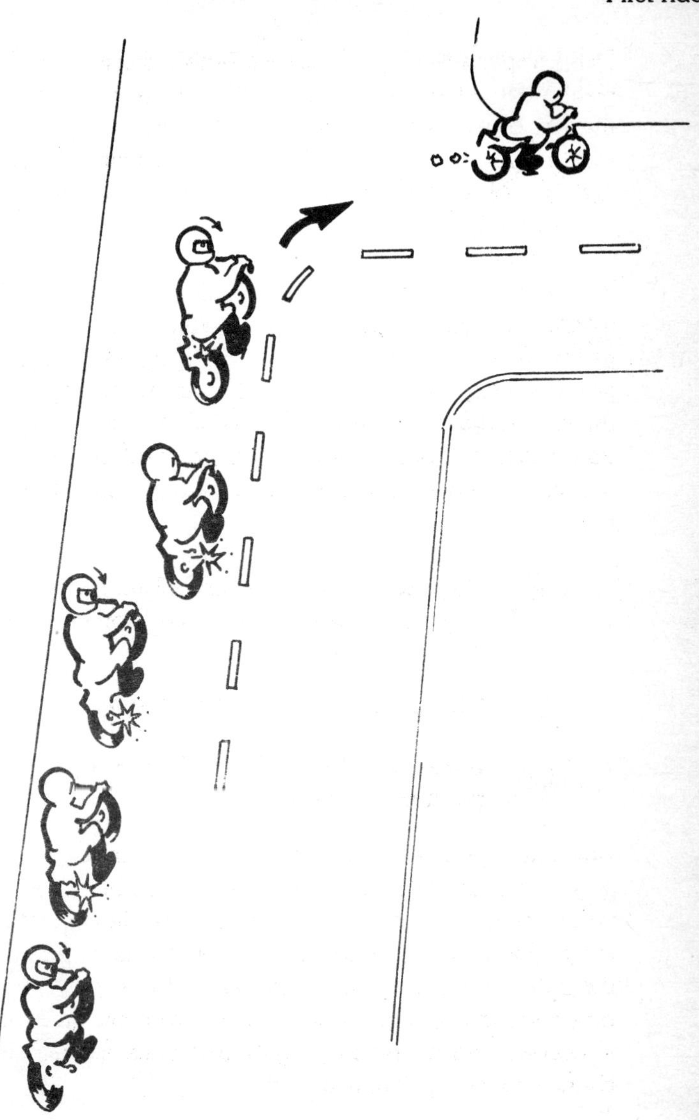

Right Turn Sequence

If you think you're going to be stationary for only a little while, then keep the bike held in first gear, covering the back brake as well, and be ready to go.

EMERGENCY STOP

Take yourself off to the other side of the training area away from your instructor and, upon his signal, set off towards him, picking up your speed and changing up through the gears. At a given point, the instructor will raise his arm and you then have to bring the bike to a stop as quickly as you can without locking the back wheel. Remember to pull in the clutch so the engine doesn't stall. Some people, usually women who have smaller hands, have difficulty in applying the front brake quickly and at the same time releasing the throttle. The result is that the bike is brought to a halt with the engine screaming. With a bit of practice on the rider's part, it should be possible to overcome this problem.

By far the biggest error committed on this exercise is locking the back wheel. This happens because when the instructor's hand goes up the rider panics and squeezes and presses too hard. Most people find it easier to get their right foot on to the back brake quicker than their right hand can reach for the front brake lever. It follows therefore that the back brake is applied first and gets pressed harder than it should. In case you need reminding, this is the wrong way round. It is the front brake that should go on first and much more pressure should be applied to that than the rear brake.

If you do lock the rear wheel, release the back brake immediately and then re-apply it gently.

Emergency Stop

And that, boys and girls, is the end of the off-road part of your CBT. You should now be taken off inside, sat down, and be told what to expect in the big wide world waiting for you outside the womb-like atmosphere of your training area.

Your instructor is obliged to brief you before taking you out on the road. As with the very first part of the CBT course, there are a number of points he must mention but most schools expand upon the syllabus. Remember the objective of the road ride. It is for you to demonstrate to your instructor that you can competently and safely apply on the road what you've been taught on the training area. Although he'd like perfection, he knows he isn't going to get it. You will be very nervous at first. There will probably be quite a few stalls, a lack of response to instructions, and all sorts of other mistakes. What he doesn't want to see though is anything dangerous. The instructor will assume that you have your own 125 cc machine waiting for you at home, even if you haven't, and that as soon as you leave his care, you're going to climb upon it and go out riding for yourself on your own. He needs to be reassured you will be safe and competent when you do.

From January 1997 this part of CBT will have to last a minimum of two hours. The DSA do insist that your ride includes traffic lights, roundabouts, junctions, crossings, hills, bends, and something called obstructions, though I'm not quite sure what they mean by that last one.

RIDE DEFENSIVELY

Riding defensively requires forethought and that is something that is usually acquired through experience. Likewise, anticipating what other people are going to do also comes with practice.

To be fair, just because you've never been on the road in any capacity before doesn't mean that you're going to come a cropper within five minutes of leaving the training area. Even if you freeze, your instructor should be your eyes and ears. I keep up an almost constant chatter, mainly because I very much enjoy the sound of my own voice.

It is an incessant monologue of 'Do this, do that, look there, watch that car, slow down, go faster' etc. I am virtually doing the riding for the trainee. It is appreciated by them because it makes them feel safer and allows time to settle their own nerves and to kick their own brain into gear. Eventually they start doing things for themselves without my prompting.

Do keep alert and awake. One of the many mistakes that novices make on the road is that they fail to look far enough ahead. Take in what's going on in front of you and act accordingly.

Use rear observation at appropriate times
This essentially means that you look behind before commencing any turn and give a Lifesaver every time you alter your course.

Assume the correct road position when riding
Keep left.

Leave sufficient space when following another vehicle
Always ask yourself this question: if the vehicle in front of you stops dead, have you left enough space for yourself to come to a comfortable stop?

Pay due regard to the effect of varying weather conditions when riding
If it's wet, slow down. If there's snow, ice, or fog about you shouldn't be on the road.

Be aware of the various types of road surfaces that can be encountered
A subject dealt with under the section on braking.

That's the official stuff that we're all obliged to throw in your direction. I have mixed feelings about it. My concern is the points and details that are omitted. For example, the DSA require that you encounter roundabouts when out on the road and yet there's no official compulsion to explain how to deal with them. So take on board the above, but read it in conjunction with what follows. What I am adding does not just pertain to your CBT road ride but also to your subsequent training and sets the standard you should be aiming for in relation to your test.

Look ahead
Let me go back to the subject of looking ahead. For many, their field of vision initially extends to perhaps 20 metres in front of them. It cannot be stressed enough that you must look ahead as far as you can see.

Nothing that happens on the road should come as a surprise to you. Bends, no matter how gentle or severe, should be noted well in advance. Traffic lights, whether green or red, should be spotted long before you get to them. You must think and concentrate all the time if you are to develop a good motorcycling brain.

It looks dreadful for a biker to have noticed a parked car so late that he has to come to a stop behind it because he can't pull out. It is one of the worst crimes you can commit. Give a right Lifesaver before pulling out and a left one before moving back in. However, keep looking ahead. If there are more parked cars a bit further on then stay out till you've passed them, and then move back in.

Staying on the subject of parked vehicles, be alert to the possibility that a door may suddenly open, putting a dangerous new obstacle in your path. Always try to keep a car door's width between you and the parked vehicle. Position yourself carefully, neither too close to the parked cars, nor in the path of the oncoming traffic. If you are on a narrow road facing oncoming traffic, then they pose the greater danger. Keep left and closer to the stationery vehicles than usual.

Traffic lights provide another example of the practical need to look ahead as you approach. Look beyond them. Are there parked cars a bit further on? If so, and if it is reasonable, position yourself to the right at the lights so you haven't got the hassle of trying to force your way out to get round them later on.

Whenever you come to a stop on the road, be it at lights or a Stop sign or whatever, before setting off again check over

each shoulder. You're looking for anything that is coming up close to you at the moment you are about to get going again. Among those things you will be looking for are pedal cyclists and pedestrians.

The same situation applies with cyclists as with pedestrians – you aren't allowed to run them over, and in fact cyclists are entitled by case law to their wobbles. So, if you come up behind one, give a right Lifesaver and then move out and give them as much room as you would a car, without endangering yourself in the process. If you're on a dual carriageway, then change lanes if it's practical. Give a left Lifesaver before moving back in.

Anyway, to continue. When you have to drop your speed or stop, look behind first. You are checking to make sure that it is actually safe for you to brake - that there isn't another vehicle so close behind you that he could hit you if you slowed down. I'm not just talking here about a situation where you'd come to a complete stop, such as at traffic lights. Take for example a scenario where a car has pulled out from a left turning on to your road and you can't move out to get round him. It'll take him a minute or so to get his speed up and he has caused you to slow. Look behind before you do so.

Another example is where a pedestrian runs across the road in front of you. You aren't going to hit him because he's sufficiently far enough ahead of you that by the time you get up to him, he'll be on the pavement. But what happens if he trips while running? Look behind anyway, even if you don't have to slow, just in case.

Give clear signals

The use of signals is an area which can cause confusion to trainees and where there may well be conflicting advice given by different instructors. I tend towards the advanced police style which is that you only signal when necessary, but I would accept the criticism that this can appear contradictory when out with trainees.

So what does signalling only when necessary mean? Well firstly, at this level of riding, *always* signal when making a turn or pulling in or moving off. Where there is an element of discretion is when you are moving out to get round a parked car or perhaps overtaking a slower-moving vehicle. In such circumstances ask yourself, 'If I put my signal on, who's going to benefit?' If there's nobody behind you for a long way then what's the point? The car in front of you that you're about to overtake needs to know? Well he might well do if you're right up his backside, but if you've judged the whole thing properly and pulled out in sufficient time, then no, he's irrelevant too.

If you come up to a slow-moving vehicle on, for example, a dual carriageway, want to get past and the traffic in the lane to your right is heavy, then yes, a signal would be most appropriate in those circumstances. Every situation is different and must be judged instantly.

Another reason for being wary of putting a signal on unnecessarily when pulling out is the possibility of other traffic assuming you're going to take the next right turn when that is not your intention. It can be tricky. On balance I would say if in doubt, put it on. Think carefully before signalling, making sure that you are not misleading other traffic.

Although you are taught a system of riding, for your own safety it must remain flexible. In a situation where you are in two minds regarding when to signal, you must decide whether the lesser of the two evils is to put your signal on early, running the risk of confusing the car behind, or to put it on very late and cause him to brake hard or take avoiding action.

Don't look down

Another very common fault when putting on an indicator is to look down to make sure your thumb has found the switch. Don't do that. You have to take your eyes off the road often enough as it is without doing it unnecessarily. Practise sitting on a stationary bike turning the signal on and off without visually checking to see you've done it right. The same applies to the horn button as well.

Use the right gear

Always, when coming to a stop, bring the machine to a halt in first gear. Change down accordingly and for the last few yards actually let the clutch out so that you know you are definitely in first. Why? Because one of the golden rules of motorcycling is that you should always be in the right gear at the right time. If, for example, you come to a halt at a stop sign in third gear, when it is clear to go you simply won't be ready – you will be in third instead of first. An examiner would take an extremely dim view of this.

Be prepared

At traffic lights, when you have stopped – in first – pause for a moment and try to gauge whether the red lights are about

to change. Look at the lights governing the traffic going in the opposite direction, that's usually a clue. If you conclude that you're going to be sitting there for a little while, then go into the *waiting position*. Do not sit holding the bike in gear as it puts an unnecessary strain on the clutch cable and is also unsafe. Suppose you let go of the clutch by accident. You'd leap forward and possibly hit the rear of the car in front. Do not however fall asleep at these lights. Many folk think that because they aren't going anywhere they can relax mentally and the concentration goes. Suddenly there will be a cacophony of car horns behind you. Your aim should be to be back in first gear and ready to go, having checked over both shoulders, as soon as the traffic lights are on green. That's green, by the way, not amber. And if you have no earthly way of judging when your lights are going to change, then guess and guess early. Don't get caught out.

The above applies if you're at the front of the queue or near it. If you're five cars back then you've got time and can move into first when you actually see your lights changing. Remember to move off with your right foot up.

And on that subject of footwork, let's have some neatness and style. Don't stop with both feet on the ground. Besides looking very untidy your right foot should have been applying the back brake. So it's the left foot that comes down, then it's the right one down as the left one comes up to put it into neutral. That then goes back down and the right one comes back up and on to the rear brake. Okay, so all of what I've just written is a blur. Re-read it till it penetrates your brain.

Footwork at traffic lights

Keep a safe distance
Remember, in general riding always make sure that you're a safe distance behind the car in front. This is something that can be easily overlooked in slow traffic situations; however it is vital to keep your distance otherwise the sudden appearance of a brake light from the car in front can be disastrous.

When you start out on your road ride be prepared to experience new sensations and experiences. You will be appalled at your sense of vulnerability. Noises in particular, not normally noticed in a car, will startle you. A windy day can blow you about. If it's raining, your visor may mist up (leave it open half an inch) and so on.

It's all jolly good fun and part of life's rich tapestry etc. but you need to be prepared for it.

Overtake safely

Overtaking can be a hoot. It may not be something that's expected of you straight away but sooner or later you're going to have to get down to it. You are expected to ride up to the speed limit as long as it's safe. You are always going to get vehicles that don't do that and trundle along quite slowly for any number of reasons. Milk floats, bicycles and people looking for somewhere to park are examples to watch out for.

Do not get too near the vehicle you plan to overtake. Instead you will have looked ahead and judged that you are going to catch them up.

 **Look Behind** to see if it is safe to move out and consider a signal. Is one necessary?

 **Signal**

 **Right Lifesaver**

 **Move out**

If you are on a dual carriageway, you will have changed lanes. If on a single carriageway, more caution is needed. Give the vehicle you are passing as much space as you can without putting yourself at risk from any oncoming traffic. Have your finger poised over the horn button just in case the driver does anything which makes you suspect he hasn't seen you. Before you have moved out in this case you will also have looked to see that there aren't any turnings ahead from which other traffic might emerge as you are in the process of

overtaking. Can you imagine the calamity that might befall you if you were overtaking and a car pulled out from a right turn as you were doing so?

Having got past, you now need to think about moving back in. Many trainees, having had drummed into them that they must keep left, get very nervous about being 'out' and try to get back in as soon as they can. This is dangerous. You must make sure there is a decent distance between the back of your machine and the front end of the vehicle you've just overtaken before you move back. A very decent distance indeed. And as such, because you have left such a space, there will usually be no need to signal left as you move in.

If you have moved back too soon and caused the car you've just overtaken to have to put his brakes on, then I would suggest that if that was a test situation then there would be a strong likelihood of a fail. Just on that. In fact any manoeuvre you carry out which has that effect on another car is likely to produce the same result.

Sometimes as you are going past, it is not unknown for car drivers to accelerate. As you will be obliged to stick to the speed limit unless something very nasty is about to develop, this can then leave you a bit high and dry. If he 'undertakes' you then that's no problem, at least not yours anyway. When he's gone you simply pull back in. It's when they end up matching your speed that you might begin to worry a bit. There you are riding along and you can't return 'home'. Relax. Just stay where you are, keeping to the speed limit, and concentrating on the road ahead. Regularly check over your left shoulder looking for a gap but don't worry if it's a while before something happens. Rest assured that some-

thing will happen and you'll then be able to move back in. Whatever you do, don't panic. If this happens to you on a test, then let me tell you with confidence that your examiner is no fool and will have seen what happened and why it did. You will not be penalised.

Pull over safely

When pulling over to the kerb whether it is to wait or to stop completely, you should follow the correct procedure:

 **Look Behind**

 **Signal left**

 **Left Lifesaver**

 **Pull over smoothly by the side of the road**

PRACTISE HILL STARTS

These may take some time to master. Go through the moving-off procedure as detailed previously. The crunch point is when you actually come to get going. Because of the incline, there is an increased likelihood of you stalling and this is the thing to avoid. People realise that they have to use a bit more throttle and are generally more cautious with the release of the clutch, but the common mistake is to forget to take the foot off the back brake. If the back brake is any good, then the result will be a stall. If it's only moderately effective, then you will ride off with the brake light on which is as good as telling the examiner that you haven't done it properly. I'm

sorry, but the trouble with motorcycling is that it not only requires you to often think about half a dozen different things at the same time, but also frequently demands of you that you do half a dozen things at the same time.

Hill Start

U-TURNS

The first thing you should do is take a good look at the road. Is there a camber? Is there a gradient? Are there parked cars about and are they positioned in such a way that they might interfere with the way you intend to do this? All these factors can have an affect on the manner in which you are seen to perform this exercise. I will come back to the relevance of these points later.

To successfully complete the U-turn, you need to apply the LSL system learned during the off road ride section of your CBT course. You are sitting on your machine in the *waiting position*, bike is in neutral, both hands on the bars, and your right foot on the back brake.

Look Behind

Signal right

Select first gear, but before anything happens, put the front brake on first. You pull in the clutch, put your right leg down, bring your left leg up and tap the gear lever down into first. You then put your left leg back down, bring your right leg back up and re-apply the back brake. You then release the front brake

Right Lifesaver and then presuming you see nothing to cause you concern, you move off. Your right signal is still on

What you have just done is gone through the correct procedure for moving off from the side of the road.

Travel fairly slowly but not so slow that it affects your stability.

After a short distance, give a **Right Lifesaver** and begin to turn. As you do so, look down and up the road. Look down the road behind you first. You should do this as soon as you have started to turn. If you were to look up the road ahead first, you would probably get a good view without having to turn your head because of the angle you would be at, at that time. But the

examiner needs to see that you are checking both ways as you are turning, so look down the road first as this will require a positive turn of the head, which he will see. By the time you have done this, the look up the road will also require a turn of the head

Do all this by the time you get to the middle of the road. This is an important point. If you leave it later, by the time you are looking forward again, the kerb on the other side of the road will be looming up at you and you could become disorientated.

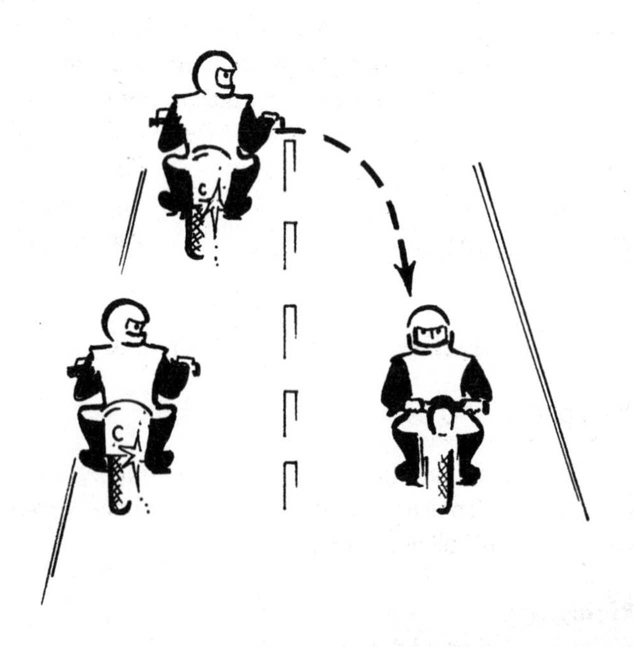

U-Turn

 **Complete the turn** and straighten up on the other side of the road, still keeping going.

 **Cancel right indicator**

 **Left indicator**

 **Left Lifesaver**

 **Pull over smoothly to the kerb**

Filter tip
One of the reasons you may have been attracted to riding a bike is because your rush hour commute is a pain in the butt and you have cast envious glances at bikers who don't appear to have been troubled by the same queue you happen to be stuck in. They have probably filtered their way along. Don't do this on your test. It is too fraught with potential danger and isn't worth the risk. If you come to a long queue, join it unless the examiner has directed you otherwise.

HANDLING COMMON OBSTACLES

ROUNDABOUTS

A lot of people find these very tricky from the point of view of when to signal and when not to and where to position themselves. It's all very simple.

Going left
Basically treat as a left turn:

 **Keep left**

Look Behind on the approach

Left Signal

On the assumption there is no traffic in front of you, as you get nearer to the roundabout look over to the right to see if there are any other vehicles already there and coming round towards you. If there are, then obviously stop, in first gear. If there aren't, then keep going. You must. Stopping unnecessarily at a roundabout is likely to lead to a test fail for not making progress. It displays a lack of confidence. Just before getting on to the roundabout, whether you've had to stop or not, give a

Left Lifesaver, keep left as you go round and give another

Left Lifesaver just before you come off. When done and dusted,

Cancel Signal and speed up

Going straight ahead

This is usually the only time when approaching a roundabout that you would not signal. As you approach:

Look Behind

Slow down using gears and brakes etc.

Left Lifesaver just before entering the roundabout. Again keep left. As you have nearly passed the left turn on the roundabout

Left Signal because if you think about it, you are now taking the next left

Left Lifesaver just before you come off and, when you've made the turn,

Cancel Signal and accelerate

Going right

A shade more complicated. Approach from the right.

Signal right. If there are two or more lanes leading up to the roundabout then you are in the right hand lane or if on a single carriageway road then to the right of that lane. You will of course have employed the procedures for the approach for a regular right turn – look behind, signal, Lifesaver, look behind, speed, gears – but instead of a right Lifesaver prior to entering the roundabout, you give a

Left Lifesaver as for the other turns. Head for the centre of the roundabout. As you have almost cleared the straight ahead exit, give a

Left Lifesaver

Signal left, move over to the left, and give a

Left Lifesaver just before you exit. And don't forget to

Cancel Signal and accelerate

Now what could be simpler than all that?

It is important when going straight on or left that you do indeed keep left. There could well be cars running parallel with you on the roundabout and we wouldn't want to upset

them or indeed our instructor by not noticing they were there and perhaps bumping into them. That would probably mean that you weren't a very good motorcyclist. What about a roundabout which has two left turns on it or three right turns, or no turns on it at all and you just end up going round and round till you run out of petrol? The same techniques apply but you use your common sense.

Take for example two left turns. If you wanted the second of the two, then you wouldn't signal on the approach but would instead do so as you were almost past the first one. If there were two right turns then you would still signal right but what counts here is when your left signal comes on, depending on which of the two rights you wanted. See?

ANIMALS

The problem of a dog running out at you, and it always seems to be a dog as opposed to any other creature, is one that is generally confined to inner city areas and so whether you are unfortunate enough to have this sort of incident occur depends really upon where you live and where you take your test.

I've no experience of accompanying a test candidate in a rural area but I suppose you could always run the risk of coming across a farmer bringing cows in for milking.

The Highway Code used to say that you should not sound your horn at an animal in case you frightened it. I never quite understood this because if I hooted at a dog that had strayed on to the road, it always had the effect of making the little chap jump out of its skin and race back towards the pavement where of course it should've been in the first place.

Now the Highway Code doesn't make any suggestion at all as to how you should behave. I would advise you to *slow down*, be prepared to actually stop if necessary, and do your best to ignore it.

Horses are a common occurrence and potentially a less hazardous one. This is because they are ridden by human beings who tend to accept the responsibility of taking an animal on to the public highway with a fair degree of *gravitas*. You do occasionally see a nervous horse but most are incredibly well-behaved. That said, never make an assumption about a horse's temperament and always give it as much room as you possibly can. You certainly will have dropped your speed. I would recommend that you don't hoot or rev your engine at a horse. A very experienced biker once told me that if he happens upon a horse suddenly, he pulls in his clutch to partially deaden the noise of the engine, and coasts past.

TRAINS

Railway level crossings are occasionally happened upon. What you do depends on the type. Most these days are governed by flashing lights, audible signals, and either full or half barriers. Believe it or not, there are still a few about with nothing but perhaps a 'Give way' sign or gates that are permanently left closed across the road so that you have to dismount and open them. With the old fashioned type you should actually come to a stop, listen to see if you can hear a train, start to cross and look both ways as you do, and then get the hell out of it. With others, treat them as unmarked crossroads i.e. look behind, slow down, look both ways, then go.

This is going to be a short chapter. There is no separate form specifically for applying for a motorcycle test. The same one as does for cars and bikes. It is called a DL 26. Before you tootle off to your post office to get one, let me stop you because you can't get them there any more.

Most training schools keep a supply of them to give out to trainees as and when required. If your school doesn't have any, look up your nearest test centre – any test centre. Go into the waiting room and pick one up from the tray on the table. If the tray is empty, go and knock on the door that says 'Private' and ask the nice man or woman who answers to give you a form.

Filling the form in is reasonably straightforward; however you can avoid it altogether if you pay by credit card over the phone. You will also get an earlier date.

You will need your card number and expiry date, and your driver number.

Box 1: Enter your driver number – the number on your licence. It begins with the first five letters of your surname. If your surname is five letters or less, then of course the whole of your surname will appear.

Box 2: Tick which type of test you require e.g. motorcycle, moped.

Box 3: Enter your name and address and phone numbers.

Box 4: State the name of the centre at which you wish to take your test . Only the test centres highlighted in bold print on the reverse of the application form carry out bike tests. You will need to consult your instructor as he may well have trained you in a specific area and might prefer you to take it there. If you're using one of your ATB's bikes then that can also have a bearing. If he's not bothered, then wherever is convenient for you.

Box 5: This does not apply for motorcycle tests and can be ignored. There ought to be a note on the form to that affect, so avoiding the confusion which often ensues.

Box 6: Here you can state preferred and unacceptable test dates. If you leave it blank, you will just be allocated the next regular date that comes up. If there are times when you won't be available then mark them in. Think carefully about ticking the box asking if you can accept a test at short notice. One might come through very quickly and you need to be sure that you're ready. Saturday tests and summer weekday evening tests are an option at a few places but they might not be available and you are likely to pay substantially more for the privilege. I once tried to book a Saturday test at my test centre which supposedly does them, and was refused because no examiner was available.

Box 7: Inform the DSA of any disabilities you might have that may effect your riding. Something like diabetes wouldn't

matter but if you're deaf they'd need to know. They'd also need to know if you can't speak English – you may be able to bring along an interpreter.

It is possible to have problems which you might not consider a disability but which could nevertheless affect your chances of success. One of the most common ones I see is a mild form of dyslexia which generally manifests itself with the trainee putting on a left signal when told to turn right and vice versa. Frequently people are not even aware that they have a problem until I point it out to them. It is nothing to be ashamed of and my advice to you would be to mention it to the examiner just prior to the test. I assure you he or she will be sympathetic and it might even work to your advantage. Likewise, I've had a couple of people recently on training who had dodgy hips and for whom kick-starting the bike was sometimes a bit of an ordeal. If you have any mild sort of problem which you think may work against you on the test, then I do urge you to speak up at the beginning of the test

Boxes 8a and 8b: These are concerned with payment. The current fee is £36 but you will need to verify that as it may well have changed by the time you come to read this.

Box 9: Complete with your signature and the date.

If you've filled the form in and sent it off, then you should get a reply within ten working days. How long you actually have to wait for your test day to roll round from when you've posted off the form will vary around the country. You should expect anything from two to six weeks if you're not looking for a short notice test. It can be longer and it just depends how well organised the DSA are in your part of the world.

You do not need to send your licence or CBT certificate in with the application form. Just make sure you turn up with them on the test date.

If you find, once your appointment card comes through, that you cannot after all make the intended test date, you will not be penalised provided you contact the DSA booking office ten working days before the set date.

If you fail to turn up and have what you consider a perfectly valid reason, illness, for example, then put your explanation in writing to the DSA and they will consider your case for another date without further payment.

NERVES

I might as well tell you now, because I won't be able to keep it a secret for too long, that I failed my test the first time, and I did so primarily because of nerves. The vast majority of my pupils, I am delighted to say, pass theirs the first time because I am able to give them the benefit of my own experience.

I was a perfectly good rider and should have passed, but I have no excuse. I was a mature man the first time I took it, someone who had been there, read the book, seen the film, got the T-shirt and so on. I was able to logically reason that my best bet was to control my nerves as best I could because my riding performance would be bound to be better, but in the end, it didn't make a lot of difference. I was unable to persuade myself of the validity of my own argument.

Everyone, and I do mean everyone, is nervous before their test; it's just that they show it in different ways. I always accompany my candidates to their test and am there for them when they get back. Consequently I am now an expert on people's behaviour in a stressful situation, and I can tell you I've seen it all. I have trained people who work in banking, marketing, the theatre, etc., all professions where people either have to sell themselves positively or where there is a

frequent demand for them to address large audiences, and still people like these are seriously nervous. At the other end of the spectrum are the few who appear calm and untroubled, but I have no hesitation in saying that they are just over-controlled and that there is inner turmoil.

There are those who just go completely to pieces mentally. I'm not saying that they break down and cry or that they are constantly shaking with fear, but their brains 'switch off'. They find they can't think or focus. I have never failed yet to get through to them, to remind them of where they are and why they are there, and then to push them out of the door only to see them reappearing some 35 minutes later wearing a great big cheesy grin.

Then there are those who are reasonably controlled before the test but collapse in a heap of mental exhaustion afterwards. I have seen people so much on edge and on a high that they have been unable to stop talking, gibbering away about all sorts of rubbish. And while I have always been too polite to comment, there have been a few occasions when standing next to a candidate after a test when I have noticed a strange smell or sudden puddle …

The reason for banging on about all this is to reassure you that if you feel or even know that you are the sort of person who might succumb to severe nerves when taking a bike test, then rest easy – the examiner will have seen it a thousand times before. There is nothing that you can do or say that will surprise him (or her). Examiners will make an allowance for nerves, though there is only so far that they can go.

So how do you overcome it? I can only tell you what you will probably tell yourself and what you already know. Don't be nervous, it's only a stupid bike test after all, not a firing squad that you're facing.

There are different approaches that you can take that might work. In January 1996 the test fee is £36. You can be sure of one thing and that is that if you are reading this some time after May 1996, if it's not £36 any more, it'll certainly not be less. To most people that's a fair sum of money, particularly when you couple it with the cost of training and clothing etc. So why give those people at the DSA another £36 because you fouled up the first time? Of course you know you're not fooling anybody with this approach, least of all yourself, but if you can adopt that attitude for 35 minutes and really believe it, then you're most of the way there.

Another approach to take is to believe that the examiner is a complete plonker who knows nothing about his job. You know more than him because you've been intensively trained over the last few weeks, and you've since read around the subject and thought about it so often and so deeply that at this level, there's not much more that anyone else can teach you. So you'll show him!

In other words – think positive!

The above should give you the general idea. If nothing that I've mentioned particularly works for you, then make your own thing up. You can be sitting on that bike with every limb twitching through nerves, but as long as you try to keep a clear mind, it doesn't matter. Dig deep within and remind yourself that you've only got to keep it together for just over half an hour.

EXAMINERS

Let me tell you that by and large, they are some of the most pleasant people you are likely to come across. They have to be and the reason they have to be is because they are doing a repetitive job and coming into contact with members of the public. If by chance you work in a shop, then you will not need me to tell you how utterly stupid a great many members of the public can be. But examiners seem able to cope with all types, probably because it's part and parcel of their profession. They are there to deal with people from all walks of lfe. In the same way that some products you can buy have built-in obsolescence, so examiners have built-in patience. I'm not saying you'll never catch one on a bad day, but if yours looks a bit dour, then just give him a great big beamy smile and I'm sure that you'll melt his heart. They do have hearts, you know.

What's more, they've all become a lot more user-friendly recently. The Driving Standards Agency, who are responsible for administering the motorcycle test, will forever in my mind be associated with the Thatcherite attitude of service and efficiency and with John Major's Citizen's Charter. This may be a totally misplaced conception on my part but that's how it happens to sit in my brain. They occasionally get things wrong and they sometimes make mistakes but the overriding impression of them is of an organisation who genuinely care about what they do and who try to do it in as an efficient and accountable manner as they possibly can within the constraints that are placed upon them. And in that drive to give the public a better service, examiners have become more relaxed and friendlier. So they say 'Good morning' and mean it. They enquire about your job and are genuinely interested. As they hand you your pass certificate they'll ask what bike you intend to get now and so on.

The other thing I admire about the examiners I have come into contact with is their utter professionalism. It took me a long time to realise just how good they are. Their standards never seem to drop or vary and in the case of a negative result, I still respect their decision. I may not like it, but I wouldn't question it.

They want you to pass. They are not looking to trick you and find excuses so that they can fail you.

Some people believe that there are quotas for test passes and that once a figure has been achieved for a week, month or whatever, then every test taken after that is a fail. This is simply not true.

Results from all examiners are analysed and if there are found to be discrepancies in pass and fail rates, then it's looked into. The motive for this is to keep examiners on their toes and to make sure there is always a uniform standard. But pass and fail quotas, no.

LOOKING THE PART

I have no factual basis for what I am about to say, but it makes common sense. Examiners don't decide to pass or fail you on the basis of your appearance; however don't turn up for your test dressed to go on the beach. Other than a helmet, there are no legal obligations regarding the clothing you wear, but I feel in my heart of hearts that if an examiner is undecided about whether to pass or fail you, the fact that you are dressed properly might just swing it. If lack of pound notes has prevented you from buying proper riding gear, then at least be seen to have made an effort. Always wear gloves of some sort, avoid trainers (boots would be better), have on a tough jacket, preferably waterproof, and a strong pair of trousers. Ideally, round it off with a Sam Browne belt or reflective jacket. Turn up wearing a short sleeve shirt, shorts and sandals and the examiner will think you're an idiot.

Try to ride with style. If you look like you know what you're doing, even if you don't, then it makes a good impression.

WHAT HAPPENS ON THE DAY

I will presume that all is in order, that the day of your test has arrived, that you have a bike and that you have all your documentation etc. Arrive at the test centre in good time. Don't get there just on the dot or a little bit late. If you've never been there before, then use your initiative and make a point of finding out precisely where it is before the day arrives. Go down there and check it out.

There will be a waiting room, and usually there is no need to let anyone know you have arrived, just plonk yourself down on a chair. Sometimes there are specific seating areas for motorcyclists and while it most certainly isn't mandatory that you sit there, I suggest you do. Pick up a magazine, bite your nails, listen to the music that is sometimes piped in, or get up and read all the official DSA blurbs that are posted around the walls. You can derive secret pleasure and amusement from watching the other people in the waiting room, because there will be others and they'll be waiting to take their car tests. Motorcycle tests are not conducted from separate premises and there is no such thing as a dedicated motor-

cycle test centre, so you have to mix with would-be car drivers and their instructors. Start to get yourself in the right frame of mind. All you're concerned about is your forthcoming test.

At the appointed time, suddenly the door will burst open and a gaggle of impeccably dressed men and women enter the room calling out various names and saying things like 'Could you sign there please' and 'Lead the way to your car'. The bike examiner appears and you'll know who he is immediately. There is an empathy among motorcyclists that often means they can recognise each other without an introduction. Of course, it also helps that your examiner will be dressed in riding gear.

Most test centres have an area outside of the waiting room where the examiner will get the candidate ready for the road ride to come. He will first ask you to sign a piece of paper which confirms that your machine is road legal (taxed, insured, MOT'd if necessary, though he does not require to see these documents). He will then ask to see your licence and CBT certificate. DON'T FORGET TO BRING THEM. From July 1996, this is mandatory and the test will not take place unless the examiner has seen both documents to check your identity and entitlements to take the test you've turned up for. Make sure your licence is signed. There will be a sign up in the waiting room threatening the fact that the test may be cancelled if it's not. Don't take the chance. Check. If your test is cancelled because of something you've forgotten to bring along, in other words if it's your fault, then you don't get a refund of the test fee. You'll be saying cheery bye to £36.

BEFORE YOU START

The examiner will compare the signature on your licence to the signature you've just put on his form. He will then start to fit the radio. These are fascinating things. They are rectangular, somewhat bulky, affairs that you wear on a belt round your waist, usually just to the front or rear of the hip. They are a very high quality piece of tackle, extremely expensive, and almost certainly nothing like the one you will have been using with your training school. There may be two ear pieces instead of the one that you normally get on the Maxons, which is the most favoured brand among bike schools, and unlike the ear piece on the Maxon which is Velcro-ed to the inside of your helmet, and which can sometimes take an age in setting up so that it is perfectly aligned with your ear, the examiner's radio ear pieces slide over your ears so that they are already in position before you put your helmet back on.

As he is fitting you up with the radio, he will ask your permission to address you by your first name. When he says that, if you can be bothered, look at his neck. You will see that around it he is wearing a somewhat tightly fitting rubber band. It is a throat microphone. When he speaks to you, he does not have to press a button, he just has to start talking and the rubber band picks up his voice from his larynx, not his mouth. Don't worry if the thought of that makes you imagine that you will hear some strange robotic mutterings; his voice will sound perfectly normal. However, because no button is pressed, the radio is vox-activated which means that the microphone kicks in when it detects somebody speaking. Occasionally it may be a bit slow to react. Having got your permission to use your first name, the examiner will always preface any instruction he gives you by using it. So if your name happens to be Robert, he will say 'Robert, take

the next left'. If the microphone is slow, you may hear 'bert, take the next left'. So you can see that using your Christian name not only puts the test on a more friendlier footing but also acts as a safety feature to make sure that you receive every instruction clearly even if the mike has been a bit slow and lopped half your moniker off. One other important thing. He can talk to you but you can't talk back to him.

He will start to give you further instructions. He will tell you that you should always presume to keep going straight ahead unless road signs dictate otherwise or he instructs you otherwise. So when you come to crossroads for example and he's said nothing, go straight over. He will tell you that should you become separated, it might be necessary for him to ask you to pull over. Should that happen, be careful where you stop. Avoid yellow lines, certainly avoid zigzag lines at a pedestrian crossing, and just generally use your brains.

He will then take you outside and ask you to read the number plate of a car that he will pick out. If you normally wear glasses then put them on. Be warned that if you can't read the number plate the test will proceed no further. Your eyesight will have been tested during CBT but it is your responsibility to make sure your eyesight is up to scratch.

Following the eye test he will remain where he is and send you over to your bike. He will say something to you over the radio to check that you can hear him properly. Be sure that you can and that you're happy with the level and the clarity. If you're not, then tell him. Now is the time to sort the problem out. He will also advise you what to do if you cannot hear him when riding. He will tell you to tap the side of your helmet with your left hand or perhaps to pull over. He

will then join you next to the bike and will ask you if it's yours. Say either 'Yes' or 'No, it belongs to blah blah training school', whichever is appropriate. He will make a note of the registration number. He will then ask you to climb on to your machine, to start the engine and to wait for further instructions. You will have left your machine on the main stand, not the side stand. Take it off properly. When the engine is going and you are waiting for directions, sit there with the bike in neutral, both hands on the bars, and the back brake on – the *waiting position*.

The examiner will then walk over to his bike and get himself ready. Very occasionally, he will use a car. There are any number of reasons why this may happen. He himself might be being subjected to a so-called 'check' test where he is being looked at to make sure he's doing his job properly. It doesn't happen very often. Some people think it's a bit naff to be tested in this way but it makes no difference to the way the test is conducted. Just put it to the back of your mind if it bothers you. Your test is now ready to commence.

THIS IS IT

The test appointment is approximately 35 minutes long. You've already taken up anything from five to seven minutes. It's beginning to look easier, isn't it? If you remove from the equation the time spent doing 'special exercises', emergency stops and so on, then you're only actually riding your bike for about 20 minutes.

So off you go. One advantage of checking out the test centre beforehand is to look at the lie of the land. Ask yourself what happens if he asks you to turn right or left or to continue

straight ahead the moment you leave the test centre. What does that bring you immediately to? Is it going to be something that in your nervous state of mind you might mess up if you're unfamiliar with it?

Which brings us to another point. Should your training school have had you go over the test routes beforehand in training? Ideally, yes. The correct answer is that it should be irrelevant. They will have taught you to ride and so you should be able to cope with anything that is thrown in your direction. The truth is that you have paid for a service and the end product is your pass certificate. If the pass rate at a training school is low, word will eventually get round and their flow of customers will drop. So they have to do whatever they reasonably can to make the test as bearable an ordeal for you as possible.

However, in most cases they are never going to be able to guarantee which route you will be on as at the majority of test centres there can potentially be a very large number of different routes. Time does not usually permit going over all of them. As long as you are broadly familiar with the general area then that should be sufficient.

It should be fairly obvious to you what the examiner's about quite soon after the test has commenced. You find yourself doing a series of left and right turns. His directions to you should come in enough time for you to prepare yourself properly.

Occasionally I have had complaints from candidates after a test that the examiner's instructions were 'nowhere near as early' as my own. It's never been a serious problem for anyone and, pass or fail, you can hardly remonstrate with him

afterwards. One other observation on this point. Some instructors, myself included, will say to a pupil, 'Go left at the lights'. Some examiners, intending you to make the same turn, will say 'Take the next left' without referring to the lights. This can cause some confusion under the pressure of test conditions so be ready for it.

A TYPICAL TEST

An examiner may vary the sequence of the test for his own reasons, but usually fairly soon after you've started, he will ask you to pull over on the left and stop the bike. He will then ask you to do an **emergency stop**. This might occur within five minutes of you leaving the test centre or as long as 15 minutes after. It just depends. In giving you the instructions for the emergency stop, he will ask you to imagine a young child has suddenly stepped off the pavement. He will also ask you to ride a left or right hand circuit. The examiners, believe it or not, broadly work to a script and in my opinion some of the phraseology they use can leave you a bit puzzled. What he means by asking you to ride a left-hand circuit is that he wants you to set off in the direction in which you are facing and to then take the first left you come to followed by the next left and the next two after that. What you are in effect doing is going round in a circle and after the last left turn, you will be back on the road from where you started. Following that last left turn, you will see the examiner standing in the road and as you draw nearer, his arm will go up. Stop the bike in as short a distance as you can, using the brakes correctly and without locking the back wheel. Don't forget to pull in the clutch so you don't stall, and I might also add that on this exercise, there is no need to change down through the gears, although some people can't help them-

selves. However, be absolutely sure that when you move off afterwards, you are definitely in first. It can sometimes be tricky finding that gear from, say third, and if you are in the wrong gear you will probably stall. You wouldn't fail your test on that point, but it doesn't look good.

The really big 'No-no' in this exercise is locking the rear wheel. If you lock the back wheel, you will almost certainly fail the test.

The likelihood of you locking the front wheel is very remote as you will be travelling in a straight line when his arm goes up. It has never happened to a candidate of mine and I do not know what an examiner's attitude to it would be. Surprised is probably the answer. However, if by some small chance you do lock the wheel, you may correct it by immediately releasing the back brake and immediately re-applying it without locking it again. It is said that if you handle the problem in this way, the examiner will not fail you. No guarantees, though.

There are some precautions you can take against failing on this exercise. As you are going round the circuit and you make the last turn back on to the road from where you started, and where the examiner is standing, watch your speed. There are some people who get 'gung-ho' about doing an emergency stop and enter into the full spirit of it by going too fast. My advice is to watch your speedo carefully and to aim for a maximum speed of 22 to 23 mph. The faster you go on this exercise, the harder it is to get right. Don't go too slowly as the examiner might feel, to put it colloquially, that you're taking the Mickey, and he could fail you for not making sufficient progress. In the unlikely event of him being

unhappy with a speed of about 22 mph, he will probably ask you to do it again, in which case you have no choice but to go faster, but still keep it under 30 mph. The chances are anyway that after the last turn, and as you are heading towards him, you won't have the opportunity to build up much of a head of steam before his arm goes up.

This brings me to three further points about this exercise. The first is that at the end of it, the examiner may well turn round to you and say, 'Thank you Robert, I won't ask you to do that exercise again'. Relax, it does not mean you've been dreadful, usually the opposite.

The second point is that in the instructions he gives you prior to you starting on the circuit, he will say to you, 'I may not ask you to perform this exercise the first time you come round'. This is in part to keep you on your toes and to prevent you from anticipating his arm going up. But the only reason his arm won't go up the first time is if there is other traffic about which might make doing an emergency stop potentially dangerous.

Thirdly, if you do foul up with a bad lock and you realise it immediately, instantly turn round to the examiner and say, 'I'm sorry, that wasn't very good, I know I can do better, I'd like to do it again please'. He'll almost certainly say no, but that's all he'll say and there's no harm in trying. If you're lucky enough to get a second shot, then make damn sure you get it right the second time.

I should point out that when you are going round this circuit, you will probably be out of sight of the examiner for a short while. Don't do anything stupid like stopping for a fag or going to fill up with petrol.

You might well wonder how far away from him you'll be when his flipper goes up. There is no set answer. A very average guide might be 20 to 30 metres but don't take that as gospel. It can and does vary. However if it's raining, expect the arm to go up sooner rather than later when your speed will be lower.

You will almost certainly be asked to perform the **U – turn** next, on the same road. When you're stopped by the examiner to commence this exercise, take a good look at the road. If there are parked cars about, they may affect how far you can travel when you move off, or how far you can travel on the other side of the road before you have to stop. Try and get your bearings. If there's a gradient, make a mental note of which way it's going. People tend to be more susceptible to 'wobble' when they have completed the turn, so if you find you're going uphill on the other side of the road however slightly, then increase your speed fractionally to maintain your stability. You may barely notice the gradient and would most certainly not consider it a 'hill', but let me assure you that your bike will definitely know that it's there.

At all costs avoid putting your foot down. Not only does it not look good but it will also probably result in a test fail. If your balance goes, then dab your foot down briefly and then get it back up straight away. Under no circumstances paddle round and neither should you stall the bike on the actual turn. Certainly, these last two points would also result in a negative test decision.

Aim for absolute control of the machine as you go round. The width of the road is obviously very relevant and is another point you should weigh up before you set off.

Overall, examiners are fairly generous in picking roads that are not too narrow. The pivotal element of control on this exercise lies with the clutch which should be gently and slowly eased over and under the biting point to either slow you down or speed you up as you are turning. This needs to be backed up by the appropriate amount of revs. The back brake should be used if any brake is required.

Standards on this exercise vary tremendously. Some people have no problem at all and are able to turn stylishly at an even speed without their hand going anywhere near the clutch or a brake being applied. Others seem constantly to run out of road or misjudge the angle or lose their balance. As long as you manage to get round, even untidily, having made sure you've given all the appropriate safety checks, then you'll be all right.

'What happens if when I start off, a car comes into view?' Cancel your right signal, pull over to the left and wait for the car to pass. Give another right Lifesaver and then begin the process all over again.

OTHER EXERCISES

While you can definitely expect to be asked to do an emergency stop and a U-turn, you may or may not be asked to do some or all of the following exercises as well. I cannot tell you why some people are asked to do certain things and others are not; however you must be prepared.

You may be asked to demonstrate a **slow ride**. The examiner will pull you over to the left and then ask you to imagine you are riding along in heavy traffic.

The object is to travel as slowly as you can, without stalling, wobbling, or putting your foot down. You will not be asked to ride like this for more than approximately 25 metres.

If you travel too fast, the examiner will simply ask you to slow down. If your clutch control is not all it should be, then don't be afraid to move off quickly at first, to avoid stalling, then regain control of the machine and bring its speed back down to walking pace.

This exercise is to see if you can control the bike at slow speed but the examiner may not ask you to perform this exercise if he has already seen you riding in heavy traffic.

During the course of your test, the examiner may ask you, possibly as many as four times, to find a safe place and **pull over** on the left. He might be specific and say, 'Stop by the next lamp post'. If not, then pick your place and think quickly. Don't stop on yellow lines or zigzag lines, try and avoid stopping just before or after a left turn, or indeed anywhere where you may cause a hazard.

 **Look Behind**

 **Signal left**

 **Left Lifesaver**

 **Pull over smoothly by the side of the road**

Initially, the examiner will be checking for good forward and rear observation. When you've stopped, he will ask you to move off again when you're ready and you should apply the moving off procedure as for the beginning of the U-turn exercise.

On one of these occasions when you've been asked to pull over on the left, you may find that you're on a hill, Not everyone is asked to do one though I do get the suspicion with my pupils that as we generally tend to practise **hill starts** on severe inclines, they expect to be asked to do one on a very steep hill on the test as well, and that they may indeed have been asked to do this exercise but have not recognised it as such.

Alarm bells should sound if on another occasion the examiner asks you to pull over on the left and to stop just behind a parked car. Stop about ten yards back. If he's not happy, he will ask you to move closer. What he's then going to ask you to do is to move off again except this time there'll be one and a half tons of Ford Mondeo in front of you. This is called an **angled start** and the object is to see if you can control the machine in a tight situation. Don't panic, all that is required is the correct moving off procedure without hitting the parked vehicle.

SUMMING UP

So where have we got to? I've told you about the formalities at the beginning of the test. I've mentioned **left** and **right turns**, the **emergency stop**, the **U-turn**, the **slow ride**, the **hill start** and an **angled start**. Let me assure you that it's taken you far longer to read all about the test so far than it will actually take you to do.

To those of you that struggle on the exercises that require co-ordinated application of the clutch, throttle and brake, may I say that you should not think that you are stupid if you have problems while your fellow trainees seem to sail

through. I can assure you it is not an indication of intelligence. Persevere and with the right instruction you will get there.

The emergency stop and U-turn are usually done one after the other, but if you are required to do any of the other exercises, you will not be asked to do them immediately after the other two. They will be spread out during the rest of the test.

You carry on riding. What you can expect depends very much on the area around the test centre. If you're in a city, then expect frequent turns, traffic lights, one-way streets, pedestrian crossings, and all the other hassle you normally get in a large conurbation. If your test centre is on the fringe of a city or in the middle of a town, large or small, then certainly expect some or all of the above but you may also get national speed limit roads as well and maybe even country lanes. You will be taken back to the test centre and when you've parked up, the examiner will take the radio off you. In the past, the examiner would have asked you some Highway Code questions, but from July 1 1996, this was replaced by a written test paper, known as the theory test. You will be exempt from this test if you already have a full licence for another category, for instance, a car.

He will then tell you whether you have passed and ask to see your licence again if the result is positive.

SOME GENERAL POINTS

SPEED

When riding on your test, get on with it. Don't think that the examiner wants to see a really cautious ride and will be greatly impressed if you take things slowly in the name of safety. He will fail you for failing to make adequate progress.

So, if you're in a 30 mph speed limit, then ride at 30 mph. It's as simple as that. By all means be cautious and drop your speed if you are passing a school, for example. *You haven't got to ride at 30 mph at any cost*. It is a question of using your brains. But if there's nothing in front of you, or if there is but as is often the case, it's breaking the speed limit and is miles ahead, then travel at 30. Look at your speedo regularly and if it's not reading 30, then ask yourself why not? And if you can't come up with a good answer, then twist that throttle.

Avoid getting caught up in the flow. Often, on a busy road where traffic is light, what cars there are about may be travelling at 40 in a 30 limit. It's easy to get drawn along. Don't. I can't repeat it often enough. Look at your speedo regularly. You will be failed for speeding but not for breaking the flow by sticking to the speed limit.

THE HIGHWAY CODE

Read it and learn it. Know your stopping distances, all the traffic signs, all the relevant bits relating to motorcycles, and all the other relevant bits in it relating to cars, bicycles, pedestrians, horse riders etc. To put it simply, if you're going to use the public highways, you should know the rules. You *can* fail

your test purely on lack of knowledge of the Highway Code. It is your responsibility to learn it.

UNMARKED CROSSROADS

I have said that examiners want to pass you and are not looking to trick you into failure. If there is one feature of the test that counters that argument then it's unmarked crossroads. Just in case you're unsure of what they are, it is a set of crossroads where there are no road markings or signs to indicate who has right of way. So the potential for a crash as two cars converge from different directions, both thinking it's OK for each to proceed, certainly exists.

This is the way to deal with them. As you approach:

Look Behind and slow right down. Be prepared to stop if necessary. As you pass through the crossroads

Look left and right. Turn your head properly so the examiner can see it. It is important to show him that you are aware of the situation you are in and are taking adequate care

Speed up and proceed

The problem with unmarked crossroads is that they can be very hard to spot until you are almost on top of them. And if you sail through one without giving the examiner any indication that you noticed it, then there's a very high probability that you will fail your test. Like on the emergency stop with the locking of the back wheel, you are dependent upon the

examiner taking a view. He may consider it to have been no problem at all if there was no other traffic about and visibility on the approach was not hampered by buildings or other obstructions. I wouldn't like to take the gamble though and I would suggest it is imperative that you train yourself to spot them and to do so early.

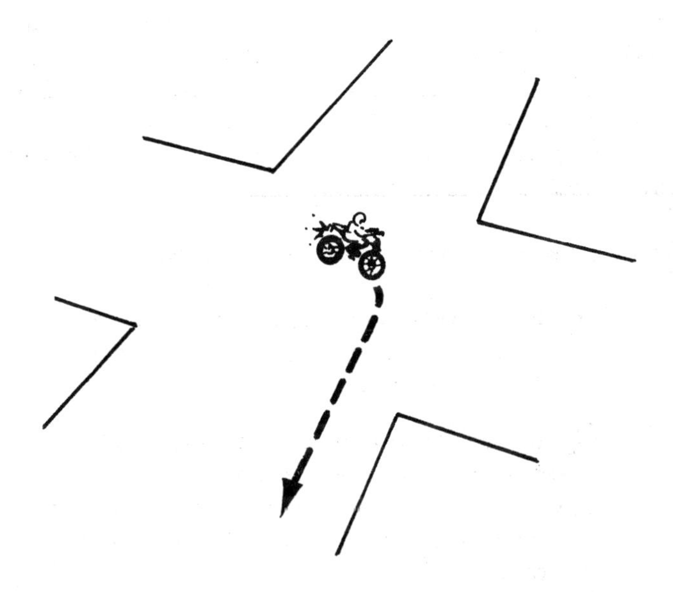

Unmarked Crossroad

Having said all that, it is by no means certain that an unmarked crossroads will crop up on your test route. But as the possibility exists, you must be prepared.

'STOP' SIGNS

When you come to a 'Stop' sign, you must stop, even if by chance you can see that your way is clear. You don't have to stop for long but your left foot should touch the ground. Failure to stop will result in an automatic test fail.

'GIVE WAY' SIGNS

You need to slow down, so look behind first. However, if you can see that the road is clear and that it is perfectly safe for you to continue without stopping, then do so. Be absolutely sure that you have looked properly, but if you can keep going, then carry on.

ZEBRA CROSSINGS

I'm referring now to an ordinary zebra crossing without any traffic lights governing it – just the usual Belisha beacons. The law says that if a pedestrian has even a foot on the crossing, you must stop. If you have time, look behind on the approach and if you think it's appropriate, also give the slowing down signal with your arm. Do not move off until all the pedestrians are fully off the crossing, even if it feels a bit ridiculous because they're well out of the way. If there's an island in the middle then you can start moving again once the pedestrians are safely on that, providing the crossing is a staggered one. Give a quick check over both shoulders before you move off. If there's loads of 'em swarming about and you're going to be there for a while, then put the bike into neutral.

If you are approaching a zebra crossing and there's someone there waiting to cross but they haven't stepped on to the crossing yet, you are not legally obliged to stop but my firm advice is that you most definitely should, because most examiners would expect you to.

If you do find you have to roll up and stop for someone, then sit there patiently and let them get on with it. Whatever you do, don't signal to them to cross. If they were to start on to the crossing as a result of a sign from you and were then to get hit by another vehicle that you hadn't noticed, then there could be problems. I know some old people can be a bit indecisive but be patient and do not rev your engine at the pedestrian. It could result in a test failure.

Zebra crossings are a fast-disappearing breed and both Pelican and even Puffin crossings are replacing them. Both these crossings are controlled by lights and you should refer to the Highway Code about the legal necessities when dealing with them. The most important point to make is that when the amber light is flashing, pedestrians still have right of way.

PEDESTRIANS

You are expected to show them courtesy and consideration.

If you see someone walking in the gutter as you approach, give a right Lifesaver and move out a bit to give them extra room. If someone's crossing a road into which you are about to turn, let them get right across it before you proceed. And always watch out at Pelican and Puffin crossings when the lights have just gone from flashing amber to green and you're about to set off – someone may step out. Watch for them and wait until they have gone.

THE EXAMINER ON THE TEST

To all intents and purposes, ignore him. Do not choose not to take an opportunity to complete a manoeuvre because you think there's only time for you to perform it but not the examiner. If he can't make the turn, he will ask you on the radio to pull over and wait for him. Do not consider whether you should or shouldn't do something because you are concerned he will not be able to follow.

LIGHTS ON OR OFF?

It's entirely up to you and the examiner's attitude towards you is genuinely not affected by what you choose to do on this point. If you are on a bike with a six volt electrical system, then my advice would be not to ride with your lights on as this can affect the efficiency of your brake light and indicators.

OTHER ROAD USERS

During your training, you will have been told to leave a safe distance between yourself and the vehicle in front. You are quite likely on your test to encounter either car drivers also on their test or learner car drivers being given a lesson by their instructors in the vicinity of the test centre. If you find yourself coming up behind anyone in a car with L-plates displayed, then leave at least half as much space again between you and them as you would with an 'ordinary' car.

KEEPING LEFT

Aim broadly to ride approximately a metre or so from the kerb unless you are travelling down a road with more than one lane going in the same direction as you, in which case you ride in the middle of the lane.

However, you are allowed to venture out, and don't be afraid to do so. Obviously you need to move out anyway to get past parked cars and the like, but don't be afraid to overtake as long as you don't break the speed limit and move back in as soon as it is safe to do so. You must give a right Lifesaver before moving out and a left one before moving back in.

And that's just about it on the test itself. On the assumption that you've passed, you can now begin to learn how to really ride. Things change. You do depend more on your mirrors and less on turning your head. Your riding position changes. You will begin to get used to being on your own, to not having someone behind you screaming in your ear and watching over you, and to thinking for yourself. And you will start to think about your riding possibly even more than before and gradually sift through the system you've been taught and discard the odd bit here and there. You will become a motorcyclist in attitude and mind and learn to regard car drivers with, at least, suspicion. Welcome to the club.

COPING WITH FAILURE

There's no getting away from it that it hurts. I cannot tell you otherwise. You will get very depressed, possibly a bit angry, and it may chew away inside you for quite some time. You might conclude that you don't want that examiner again, however you have no choice. It is even possible that if you elect to go to another centre for the re-test that he'll be there too. Alternatively you may decide that you can't wait to get back and show the 'berk' that he was wrong. Unfortunately, failing a test is all part of the rich fabric of life.

Look at your failure sheet and the boxes that the examiner has marked. Is it one obvious mistake of a serious nature which you knew about the moment you made it or was it a series of things? Show the sheet to your instructor who should ask you to try to recall the incidents that caused the errors. Are they mistakes that you normally make when riding or was it all caused due to the pressure of the situation? There are many questions you need to ask yourself if you fail so that you can work on the answers with further training. I know that sounds a bit pat but that is the only answer.

If, for some reason, you genuinely feel you've been hard done by, you do have a right of appeal but its terms of reference are very narrow and the examiner's decision will not be reversed. It is more a channel for making a complaint if you feel the examiner has behaved badly or, in your opinion, has made a mistake. Frankly, it's not worth it.

SOME HIGHWAY CODE QUESTIONS

These examples below are in addition to any questions that may be put to you on road signs or stopping distances. They are only examples and by no means the extent of the potential range of questions that could be included in the test.

What's the maximum permitted speed limit for a motorcycle on a dual carriageway?

Tricky because of the use of the word 'motorcycle' which implies it's different from cars. It isn't. 70 mph is the maximum speed for all vehicles although it may be 40, 50 or 60 mph.

What is the correct procedure for joining a motorway?

When on the slip road look over your right shoulder to gauge the volume and speed of the traffic, consider a signal, and bring your own speed up so that it matches that of the traffic already on the motorway.

What advice would you give to someone who was going to ride pillion with you?

Don't be smart and say 'Don't'. The three salient points Mr. Examiner wants to hear are: the pillion must keep his feet on the foot pegs, he must wear a legally-approved helmet, and that helmet must be done up.

What parts of a motorcycle can be adjusted to suit an individual rider?

Suspension, foot pegs, seat, mirrors.

Why is it necessary to maintain correct tyre pressures?

If the tyre pressures are wrong it can lead to unsafe handling or excessive tyre wear.

Which is the most important brake on a bike?

Front brake.

How would you stop a bike in an emergency?

They only seem to want the answer for dry conditions which is front brake on fractionally ahead of the back brake and 75

per cent effort via the front. You could add, if given the opportunity, that in the wet both brakes would be applied simultaneously and with equal pressure.

What items on a bike would you check before commencing riding?

The first thing I'd do would be to check I had sufficient petrol. Then I would look at my tyres. I'd check for pressure and general wear and tear. I'd make sure there were no nails or other foreign bodies embedded in the rubber and that they had at least the legal minimum depth of tread. Then I would look at my chain and check it for tension – adjusting it if necessary, and I would also make sure it was sufficiently lubricated. Next I would look at my oil level and would top it up if required. Then I'd take a look at the electrics. I'd ensure all the lights were working, replacing any bulbs that had gone, that my indicators were functioning correctly, and that my horn worked. I'd make sure that when a brake was applied, front or back, that the brake light came on. I would test the brakes themselves to ascertain that they were working properly and would adjust them if appropriate. I would measure the battery level and top it up if needed. I would take out the spark plug and clean it with an Oral B toothbrush (I find Oral B best for this task because of the curved head which enables the bristles to get into all those cute little spots that spark plugs are inclined to have). I would also re-set the gap if necessary. I'd check my gearbox oil level as well as the water level in the radiator and the brake fluid level too, topping up when necessary. I'd examine the clutch and throttle cables, making sure they operated smoothly and had no kinks in them or frayed bits. I'd have a damn good look at the exhaust, making sure nothing was rattling, that

there were no holes in it and that it was free from rust. I'd make sure my mirrors were clean and correctly aligned ...

You could ramble on for hours in far more detail than I've gone into here, but just saying petrol, lights, indicators, oil, chain, tyres is probably sufficient.

What changes in the roadsurface should a motor cyclist be on the look out for?

Covered in section on braking. So go back and look it up. Clue: it starts on pg 69.

How would you ride in fog?

First, ask yourself if your journey is really necessary. Put on lights, drop speed, increase distance between yourself and vehicle in front, don't be inclined to follow the tail lights of the car in front.

What do white lights on the back of a car mean?

The vehicle is in reverse gear.

Which lane would you normally ride in on the motorway?

Lane One – the inside lane.

What would you do if you missed your exit on a motorway?

Carry on to the next one.

When can you enter a yellow box?

When your exit ahead of you is clear or when waiting to turn right.

What does a flashing amber light at a pedestrian crossing mean?

You may proceed but pedestrians on the crossing still have right of way.

'I've passed my test thank you Stuart. Your book was a great help. I've now bought my own bike and I want more. I want to continue an active involvement in motorcycling beyond just being a rider. What do you suggest?'

There are a number things you can do. The first is to go back to your ATB and ask if they need another instructor! That is of course if the idea appeals. Don't expect any pay to begin with but do expect to be given the least attractive jobs. It will all be off-road work until you've held a licence for two years.

If you want to improve your skills further, then consider doing an advanced course. There are plenty of commercial organisations offering these sorts of schemes. Your own ATB may even run one. By this stage you will have been able to gauge for yourself how good they are. But for the best value for money and for general dedication to the cause you should try the Institute of Advanced Motorists.

Their headquarters are in London and the phone number is 0181 994 4403. They will pass on the number of the secretary of your local motorcycle group. The bike groups are populated by members who tend to be out-going people who have a genuine belief in the promotion of road safety. They will not rush it but they will train you to a higher, more

thoughtful and intelligent standard of riding, often with police assistance. There is a test to aim for, which is usually conducted by a police Class One rider, and the end result is a certificate and membership of the Institute.

You could also join your local bike club. Many are affiliated to the British Motorcyclists Federation and a call to their headquarters will get you all the details.

Once you have successfully passed your test, I have one extra piece of advice. Start to learn again. I know this is patronising and I'm going to sound like every other duffer in your life who's talked down to you before. But from now on there'll be no instructor riding behind and no voice in your ear. You're on your own. Apply what you've learnt but question it as well. Don't take a lazy approach. Instead take an intelligent, enquiring attitude. Adapt your system of riding gradually. Aim for smoothness, good anticipation, far-sighted forward observation and, most importantly, safety. Above all, enjoy it.

MOTORCYCLES

RESTRICTIONS ON LEARNERS

Minimum age 17. Maximum sized machine 125 cc, maximum power 12 bhp. and 14.6 bhp from January 1997.

PROVISIONAL LICENCE WITH MOTORCYCLE ENTITLEMENT

If this was issued before December 1 1990, you do not have to do CBT first in order to ride on the roads but you must display L-plates and pass your test within two years. You do have to do CBT prior to taking the test. You can re-take the test as many times as you need to within that two year period but if you fail to get through, you have to stop riding motorcycles for 12 months. You can however switch to a moped without any time penalty. Once you've passed, you can throw your L-plates away, and you can carry a pillion. Good luck.

If your provisional licence was issued after December 1 1990 then all the above applies to you as well but you must do CBT first before riding on the road.

FULL CAR OR MOPED LICENCE

If either of the above were obtained before December 1 1990, then you can ride on public roads without doing CBT first (though I wouldn't advise it). If you want to take the test then you have to do CBT. If you fail there's no real problem. You are not banned from riding motorcycles for 12 months after two years.

From January 1997 this facility will be withdrawn to full and provisional car licence holders with a pre-December 1990 licence. You will have to do CBT first before riding on the road.

If your full licence was obtained after December 1 1990, then all the above applies to you too except that you must do CBT first before riding on two wheels on the road.

No matter what licence category you fall into, bear in mind that from January 1997 a CBT certificate is valid for only three years. If you haven't passed the test within that time then you'll need to do it again. Note also that a CBT certificate obtained on a moped is valid for a learner-legal motorcycle.

MOPEDS

RESTRICTIONS ON LEARNERS

Minimum age 16. Maximum sized engine 50 cc and top speed 30 mph.

PROVISIONAL LICENCE WITH MOPED ENTITLEMENT

If issued before December 1 1990, then no need to do CBT first but you will have to do it if you want to take the moped test.

If your provisional licence was issued after that date, then CBT must come first.

FULL CAR OR FULL MOTORCYCLE LICENCE

No matter when you obtained your licence, you have complete moped entitlement – no need for L-plates.

Once you have passed the moped test, you can, if your machine is so fitted out, carry a pillion. You are not allowed on motorways. Note: On a provisional moped licence you are not restricted to the two year limitation. You can ride forever without taking the test as long as you display L-plates.

CHANGES

CHANGES TO LICENCE REQUIREMENTS FROM JANUARY 1 1997

If you're aged between 17 and 21, nothing much changes in terms of the test, the way it's conducted and how you train for it. The difference starts after you've passed. For the first two years of your full licence, you are restricted to a machine no more powerful than 33 bhp. That very roughly translates to something between 300 cc and 500 cc. Very roughly indeed.

All the major manufacturers will be introducing 33 bhp versions of existing models to fulfil the inevitable demand.

People over 21 years old don't have to wait two years to ride a big bike (although you do have that option).They have the option of Direct Access. This involves training for your test and taking it on a machine producing not less than 46.6 bhp.

CBT can be taken by Direct Access riders on any machine. You can, if you prefer, however take your CBT on a 125 and progress on to a larger bike for post-CBT training. The new rules mean you could take your test on a Harley, a Honda Fireblade, or literally any machine. It is possible that your test, though no longer in duration, may encompass different types of road to allow for the greater performance of your bike.

All training on Direct Access must be carried out on a two to one ratio. This is likely to lead to greater costs than at present. Whether you use your own bike or a training school's, it will have to display L-plates and you will not be allowed out on your own. You must always be accompanied. The road ride element of all CBT courses will have to last for a minimum of two hours although this will not have to be done in one session. There must be a radio link between the instructor and trainee. The instructor will have had to have undergone a special training course to enable him to conduct Direct Access training, so make sure your instructor is appropriately qualified.

Should you have passed your test when aged under 21, you can, if you wish, go on to Accelerated Access when your 21st birthday rolls around. This will get you on to a bigger bike

without the two year delay. You won't have to do CBT again, but you will have to take another test on a larger machine and the rules that apply to Direct Access will apply to you as well.

I said earlier that if you're between 17 and 21 nothing much changes as regards the test. 'Nothing much' is broadly correct. Before January 1997, you are entitled to take your motorcycle test on anything as long as it is bigger than a 50 cc moped and no bigger than a 125 cc machine pushing out a maximum of 12 bhp. You could therefore take it on a RXS 100, a C90, a Townmate, etc. Not after January 1. The test must be taken on a bike over 120 cc but no bigger than 125 cc and capable of at least 61 mph. The current 'bog standard' learner-legal 125 would still suffice. Just to make matters more complicated, the maximum power a 125 can produce is increased from 12 bhp to 14.6 bhp. That has little bearing though and the pre-July 1996 learner-legal 125 cc machines will continue to be valid test bikes.

What happens to those that don't want to ride a moped but likewise don't want anything bigger than a 125? Oh praise be, for a new licence category has been specifically created for you, you lucky souls. It is called the A1 Light Motorcycle Licence. Your CBT and training is the same as it currently is pre-July 1996 but your test must be taken on a machine of between 75 and 120 cc. However, having passed, you can then ride a bike up to 125 cc producing 14.6 bhp. Small sting in the tail. If you take the test on a bike with automatic transmission then you can only ride automatic machines afterwards.

THEORY TEST

The other big change from July 1 1996 is the introduction of a new theory test. This is not an anti-biking brickbat and will apply to all new car drivers as well. It will replace the Highway Code questions currently thrown at you at the end of the test. These theory tests will probably be conducted at schools and other educational establishments, possibly in the evening, and will be contracted out by the DSA to a private sector organisation. Of course, there will be an additional fee.

In order to sit the theory exam, you will need to hold the relevant provisional licence appropriate to the riding test you intend to take. Once the scheme is fully operational, you will have to pass the theory test before applying for your practical test. For the first six months after its introduction, however, you can choose which to do first. You must complete both parts of the test, the theory and practical, within two years otherwise a test pass will lapse and will have to be re-taken.

The theory paper will be similar for both car and bikes. So if you pass your car test and then want to go on to learn to ride a bike, you will not have to re-sit the exam. Likewise if you pass your bike test first and then go on to learn to drive a car. In other words, you will only have to take it once even if you're taking another test to upgrade the bike you can ride.

As for the theory test itself, it will last for about 30 minutes and will consist of approximately 35 multiple choice questions from an overall potential pool of 600. Most of the questions (with the possible exception of 'What is your name?') will require you to select the correct answer from four options. You will need to get 26 correct answers to pass.

The topics that will be covered are as follows:

Alertness Concentration, anticipation, observation, awareness, distraction, boredom

Attitude to other road users Consideration, close following, courtesy, priority

Vehicle defects, safety equipment and the environment Mechanical defects, detection and understanding implications for safety, safety equipment, fuel consumption, pollution (including noise) regulations

Weather and road conditions Safety margins and effect of weather and road surface conditions, visibility

Mental Impairment Alcohol, fatigue, medication, drugs, stress, ill-health, ageing, sensory impairment, regulations

Perception Information processing, attention, scanning, identification of hazards, time to detect hazards, interpretation

Judgement and decision making Appropriate action, interpretation, reaction time, speed, distance

Other road users Elderly drivers, motorcyclists, new drivers, vulnerable road users

children, pedestrians, cyclists, disabled people, lack of traffic experience

Other vehicle characteristics
Motorcycles, lorries, buses, manoeuvrability, field of view, braking distances, acceleration/performance, slip streams, road surface spray

Own vehicle handling Effects of: weather, road conditions, time of day, lighting, traffic calming, speed

Roads and regulations – motorways
Limitations: speed limits, lane discipline, parking, lighting

Roads and regulations – other roads
Limitations: speed limits, lane discipline, parking/clearways, lighting

Signs and signals Road traffic regulations regarding road signs, markings, signals, rights of way and speed limits

Documents Rules concerning administrative documents required for use of vehicles

Accident handling Use of first aid kit and other first aid precautions, setting warning device, raising alarm, police reporting procedures, witness responsibilities, regulations

Vehicle loading Safety factors concerning vehicles and persons carried, stability, towing regulations

Accident risk Relative risk for different road user groups, situations/contexts, impairment, road types, speed and severity

If you've managed to read all the way through that then you're probably appalled and think you'll need a six month foundation course just to prepare. I hardly think you'll need to worry. I'm quite sure a thorough reading of the Highway Code will get you through. If you are still concerned, the DSA is planning to publish a booklet dealing with the test and listing selected questions.

In February 1996, the rule stipulating that you must wait one month before re-taking a test was abolished. You can now fail on a Monday and pass on Tuesday!

I find it amusing to observe the attitude and approach of trainees, while they are learning, towards what they intend to ride after they've passed their test. Some, a sizeable minority, have already bought or acquired a bike which is either waiting at home in the garage or is sitting in storage at a bike dealer. Others say, 'I'll be getting a so and so' but most just haven't got a clue. People change their minds frequently during training and can often end up with completely different ideas on what they intended to buy.

The first question you must ask yourself is, 'What do I want a bike for?' Generally, bike usage falls into three categories:

 **Commuting** – to work or college

 **Pleasure** – riding at the weekend etc.

 **Touring** – long distance travel in the UK or abroad

There are plenty of machines around that fulfil each specific application. But no doubt you are an awkward individual who has glanced through the above list and said to yourself,

'I want a bike that can do all three'. Well you would, wouldn't you?

And therein lies the rub, because bike buying is often a compromise, with the machine having to be capable of dealing with all manner of demands placed upon it.

It does pay, however, to broaden your mind and to be prepared to be flexible. Let us say for example that you are in your late teens and live in the great Metropolitan Elysium of Manchester. Let us further presume that you are a manic depressive who has lost all sense of reality and have decided that for the purposes of your further education you would be better off going to an urban University in Liverpool, a distance of some 38 miles. Because of your fragile mental condition, you prefer to live with Mum and Dad and hence you are required to make a daily round trip of some 76 miles. Also because of your mental state you have a strong ethereal side to your personality which manifests itself in your fondness for spending time inside post-1978 German Cathedrals, and you take the opportunity to do this during the long summer break. You have learned to ride a bike so as to have an economical and efficient means of getting over to Merseyside but would also like to use it to get over to Germany for two weeks of the year.

A bike that would more than adequately cope with the commute is the Honda CB 250. (I pick on this purely for the sake of selecting an example but there are loads more machines that would easily fall into this category.) It would be fine for getting to Liverpool and back every day, but Hanover? On a 250? And why not? Because it'll certainly get you there. Not as quickly as a larger bike, not as comfortably or with as

much luggage but get you there it will. Providing you have the right mental attitude and are prepared to be restricted to travelling at somewhere between 60 to 70 mph and perhaps to be exposed to the vagaries of the weather a bit more, then it will adequately do the job.

If you still have no specific idea of what you want, then buy one of the glossy monthly bike mags that contain pictures of every new machine currently on the market. In general terms there are few quality and reliability differences between the big four Japanese importers, and Triumph's reputation is now reasonably well re-established.

You may hear of something called grey imports. These are second-hand bikes usually built specifically for the American or Japanese domestic markets and not available here. They started coming into the country a few years ago in response to the increasing cost of new bikes made for the UK market. People wanted something different and cheaper. When they first started appearing a lot of fuss was made. There were claims that they didn't comply with UK specification, that there'd be insurance problems and that parts would be very difficult to get. Most bike dealers offering grey imports these days sell low-mileage machines backed up by a warranty and a good stock of spares. They can be worth considering.

There are some who, no matter what their financial standing, always buy second-hand even if they can afford to buy new. If you decide to go down that path, where should you look? The golden rule is, if you go to a dealer you will pay quite a bit more but you will probably have the fallback of a warranty of some sort. If you buy privately you are taking more of a risk.

If you know nothing about what to look for when buying a second-hand motorcycle, then take someone along who really does. A mate is all very well but does he really know what he's talking about or is it all hot air? Take someone who is actively involved in bike repairs. Offer to pay them. It is far better to end up paying £60 for having dragged someone along to view three bikes with you than to have bought a machine on your own because it looks all right, only to discover £300 worth of repair work is needed.

You should find out locally where people tend to advertise second-hand machines. Wander into a large newsagent and take a look at magazines like *Loot* and *Motor Cycle News*. If you're fortunate enough to have an edition of *Loot* covering your area then that tends to be ideal as the advertised machines will be relatively local. The problem with *MCN* is that your ideal bike could be 400 miles away.

One of the reasons why your bike insurance might be relatively high is that motorcycle theft has become a major professional crime. This results in an abundance of claims to insurance companies and ensuing higher premiums. These stolen bikes, unless taken for the thief's own personal use, have to be sold on otherwise there isn't a lot of point in nicking them in the first place. Some of these bike thieves are so unbelievably dumb that it's staggering. Ask to see the log book of any machine you intend to buy. If it's back at Swansea because he's just bought it and is getting his name put on it or if you're given some other pathetic excuse, then, no matter how plausible it may sound, that, as far as you're concerned, is as far as this particular transaction goes. Bid the vendor a fond farewell.

If the log book is produced, be apologetic but look for the little plate on the bike with the chassis number stamped on it and make sure it tallies with the one on the log book. If the chassis number is indecipherable because someone has attempted to file it off, make your excuses and leave.

If everything above seems right, then proceed. Remember, a bike doesn't have to have an MOT. Of course it must if it's over three years old and is going to be ridden on the road, but no offence has been committed if the owner has kept it stored for, say six months and the MOT has expired. Likewise, whether it's insured or not is irrelevant to you.

You will need to make sure that any used bike you buy does have an MOT which you will be responsible for getting if you buy it without. You will also need to get it insured and taxed – unless the machine is more than 25 years old in which case it is exempt from road tax.

A dealer will probably let you test ride a machine and ideally a private seller should do the same. However, be sympathetic to the latter's discomfort when you ask the question. After all, what's to stop you climbing on and riding off? Bring along convincing proof of identity, such as a passport, and be prepared to leave something behind.

Haggle over price. Make an offer. If you're a bit shy in that direction, remember it's your money and even £20 saved is better than nothing.

If you've got no money or very little, then consider borrowing. You will of course need a regular income to convince the lender that you are able to repay the loan. If you are out of work or are still in further education, then I've got to be honest and say that your options are limited.

The cheapest way of borrowing is from parents, friends or other private sources. Next is a bank overdraft, but a bank is unlikely to give you one of these purely for the purchase of a motorcycle. They will probably steer you towards a personal loan. Bike dealers also have finance facilities even for second-hand machines, and it will be up to you to look out for the best deal. If you are a terrible risk and are frequently turned down, then you might consider making the purchase on a credit card if you have one and the limit is high enough. But you'll only have luck with this at a dealer and remember, it does have to be paid back.

INSURANCE

On the subject of insurance, the best method of attack on this matter is to refer to the appropriate classified section in *Motor Cycle News*. There is a large list of brokers specialising in bike insurance every week. Do not be put off ringing them by the fact that they may be on the other side of the country. Make a number of calls. The chances are that by the third or fourth you may be getting a familiar story but persevere. Chances are you'll end up with Norwich Union in one form or another anyway as they have the lion's share of the UK market. Don't feel obliged to go to your local insurance broker because he plays golf with your dad and has been looking after your family for the previous 300 years. He may not specialise in bikes and you may end up paying well over the odds.

Index